Warrior's Admonition

Your body is your temple: Care for it!
Do not engage in useless activity.
Listen to the Goddess.
Help thyself.
You create your own reality.

The Warrior's path is creativity.
A serene path to enlightenment.
Know thyself.
Master thyself.
Create your own reality.

Nurture the ability to perceive the truth in all matters.
Perceive that which cannot be seen with the eye.
Learn from your mistakes.
Teach thyself.
Create your own reality.

Do not be negligent, even in trifling matters.
Grace and guilt do not exist:
Strive for responsibility.
Honor thyself.
Create your own reality.

Never disgrace the Goddess, the God, nor Wicca.
Do not harbor sinister designs.
Harm none, do what thou wilt.
Master thyself.
Create your own reality.

About the Author

A former Air Force officer, Kerr Cuhulain (Vancouver) has been a police officer for the past twenty years, and a Wiccan for thirty. He is one of the few publicly Wiccan police officers in the world. He's served on a SWAT team, Gang Crime Unit, and hostage negotiation team. He travels throughout North America as a popular speaker at writers' conferences and Pagan festivals, and he has been the subject of many books, articles, and media interviews. He is author of *Wiccan Warrior* and *The Law Enforcement Guide to Wicca*.

To Write to the Author

If you wish to contact the author or would like more information about this book, please write to the author in care of Llewellyn Worldwide and we will forward your request. Both the author and publisher appreciate hearing from you and learning of your enjoyment of this book and how it has helped you. Llewellyn Worldwide cannot guarantee that every letter written to the author can be answered, but all will be forwarded. Please write to:

Kerr Cuhulain
℅ Llewellyn Worldwide
P.O. Box 64383, Dept. 0-7387-0254-4
St. Paul, MN 55164-0383, U.S.A.

Please enclose a self-addressed stamped envelope for reply, or $1.00 to cover costs. If outside U.S.A., enclose international postal reply coupon.

Many of Llewellyn's authors have websites with additional information and resources. For more information, please visit our website at
http://www.llewellyn.com.

Full Contact
Magick

A BOOK OF SHADOWS FOR THE
WICCAN WARRIOR

Kerr Cuhulain

Author of *Wiccan Warrior*

2002
Llewellyn Publications
St. Paul, Minnesota 55164-0383 U.S.A.

FIRST EDITION
Second Printing, 2002

Book design by Michael Maupin
Cover design by Gavin Dayton Duffy
Photo of Kerr Cuhulain by permission of Sarah Murray (www.smurrayphoto.com)

The following publisher has generously given permission to use extended quotations from the following copyrighted work: *The Millionaire Next Door* by Thomas D. Stanley and William D. Danko, Longstreet Press and Pocket Books © 1998.

Library of Congress Cataloging-in-Publication Data
Cuhulain, Kerr, 1954 –
   Full contact magick : a book of shadows for the wiccan warrior / Kerr
     Cuhulain. — 1st ed.
      p. cm.
   Includes bibliographical references (p.) and index.
   ISBN 0-7387-0254-4
     1. Witchcraft. 2. Self-realization—Miscellanea. 3. Neopaganism. 4. Self-realization—Religious aspects—Neopaganism. I. Title.

   BF1566 .C825 2002
   133.4'3—dc21   2002072907

Llewellyn Worldwide does not participate in, endorse, or have any authority or responsibility concerning private business transactions between our authors and the public.
   All mail addressed to the author is forwarded but the publisher cannot, unless specifically instructed by the author, give out an address or phone number.
   Any Internet references contained in this work are current at publication time, but the publisher cannot guarantee that a specific location will continue to be maintained. Please refer to the publisher's website for links to authors' websites and other sources.

Llewellyn Publications
A Division of Llewellyn Worldwide, Ltd.
P.O. Box 64383, Dept. 0-7387-0254-4
St. Paul, MN 55164-0383, U.S.A.
www.llewellyn.com

Printed in the United States of America

Also by Kerr Cuhulain

The Law Enforcement Guide to Wicca
(Horned Owl Publications, third edition, 1997)

Wiccan Warrior
(Llewellyn Publications, 1999)

Dedication

This book is dedicated to the unsung heroes who use their Warrior spirit to achieve personal victories in overcoming handicaps and adversity. Sometimes this recognition is public, as it was in the case of my dear wife Phoenix McFarland, who overcame traumatic brain injury (TBI) to become a published author and performer. Another survivor of TBI is Grian Redlion. I'm told that, due to his brain injury, Grian has trouble expressing himself. But his Warrior spirit certainly shone through when he shared the following note with me on Lughnasad 2000:

> *The warrior is noble with the conviction that heroes are made of . . . The warrior would fight not to win, but to be free, for that is the grand prize. Everything else will follow. The Wiccan Warrior is human, though not perfect. He/she tries to treat each person with kindness and respect. The warrior rolls with the punches and attacks and even says to you, "Be blessed my brother or sister." The Wiccan Warrior can take a whopping and use it as a . . . lesson and knows not to become hard and bitter in attitude through meditation . . . The Wiccan Warrior will fight with no stain. The warrior is passionate and a deep thinker who is true to the God and Goddess and everything that is sacred. The Wiccan Warrior can smile because the Warrior is a Witch and . . . appreciates everything and takes nothing for granted . . . A Wiccan Warrior is a person who cares, is compassionate . . . and an observer of all things great and small. He is provider, lover, sensual, strong, fragile, determined and open minded. A great Wiccan Warrior is all these things and more to be a Wiccan fighting for justice, compassion, understanding, and no fear.*

Grian Redlion, Wiccan Warrior

Acknowledgments

I'd like to thank my old friend Fritz Muntean for his many discussions with me that proved to be fertile fields of the imagination. I'm grateful to Wiccan author Phyllis Curott for her discussions with me at BBMMDC, which helped me focus some of my ideas. I have a large group of people that I'd like to thank for the rite of passage for Jade: Delia Stone (one of the participants) for bringing it to my attention in the first place, and Sandra Zack for letting me include her rite of passage for Kimberly Chagnon (Jade) in this book. It is a wonderful ritual and I'm glad that she could share it with me and my readers.

My thanks to the many Wiccan police, medical, and rescue personnel on Lady Kiara's "Officers of Avalon" e-group for their companionship, encouragement, and thoughts. Special thanks to Officers of Avalon member Marco Rodriguez of the LAPD for his thoughts on tools and magick. My thoughts go out to Rick Allen (aka "Lord Spam") of the PCCO who passed on to the Summerland. We'll miss your humor and your energetic rituals. My thoughts also go out to my friend and fellow Warrior Paul Tuitean, who also passed on to the Summerland this past year. My early discussions with Paul were what got me thinking of developing this Warrior system for Wiccans in the first place.

Eternal thanks to my wife and best friend Phoenix McFarland for inspiration, encouragement, and putting up with the long hours that I spent hunched over my computer creating this book.

Contents

Book Four – The Book of Fire

Book Five – The Book of Air

Preface

THERE IS AN old saying in Karate: Chi ("energy", pronounced "chee") follows I ("intent," pronounced "eee" to rhyme with "see"). This is also a definition of magick: "Causing change by directing energy with one's will." Since the perfect striking technique is 80 to 90 percent chi, one could say that martial arts are really full contact magick. Obviously this energy is accessed instantaneously and without the need for ritual or tools. It wouldn't be of any use to the martial artist if you could not. This book is not about martial arts or fighting, it is about accessing magickal energy instantaneously. You won't have to join a dojo, but you will have to do some homework.

This is a book of practical magick. If you picked up this book looking for some way to take control of your destiny, you've come to the right place. It is a book about accessing your internal energy and strength in order to put some direction in your life, to find a way to overcome obstacles and problems in your life, to heal yourself mentally and emotionally, or just to know yourself better. This book will help you to access your natural gifts.

If you just picked up this book looking for information on Satanism, put it back on the bookshelf. You won't find Satan in these pages. Satan is a bogeyman created by the Church to scare people into the pews. Wiccans don't believe in bogeymen.

Likewise, if you picked up this book looking for destructive magick for revenge or domination, put it back. There is nothing destructive in this book. Being a Wiccan and a Warrior is about empowering yourself and achieving your dreams, not about dominating others.

I am a Warrior and I am a Witch. Either one of these "W" words conjure up negative images for some people. This is because many different people use these two words to mean many different things. The confusion is also partially due to the proliferation of urban legends about Satanism and the occult. This is also partially due to the glorification of violence in theaters and on television. So let me start by explaining what I mean by these terms.

The word Wicca, from which the word Witch is derived, can be traced back 8,000 years to the proto-Indo-European root word *weik* (pronounced "way-ick"), which means "pertaining to magic and religion."[1] This eventually became the word *wicca* (pronounced "wee'cha") in Old English. "Wicca" translates as "male sorcerer," while the word "Wicce" was the Old English word for a female sorcerer. In modern usage most Wiccans pronounce "Wicca" with a hard *c* and use the term to refer to both male and female followers.

As the etymology of the word Wicca suggests, Wicca is a religion of magick. You'll note that I spell the word magick with a *k*. I do this to distinguish it from "magic," the sleight-of-hand tricks also known as legerdemain used by entertainers. This book isn't about magic. It is about a life-affirming religion based in nature. People are drawn to this magickal religion for many reasons. Some seekers are looking for magick that can turn their situation around. If you are one of these people, then this book is for you. Some seekers come to Wicca to find a religion that reconnects them with the natural world and the turning seasons. If this is what you are looking for, then you've just arrived at your destination.

Like Buddhism, Wicca is a religion of practice, not a religion of creed. Wiccans are "producers of religion, not merely consumers."[2] Wiccans make a commitment to create and conduct rituals, teach and mentor others, and produce positive works. Everyone is clergy. Wicca is not merely a social activity for me. It is my everyday path through life.

When I use the term "Warrior," I'm not referring to a soldier, a combatant, or a man-at-arms. A Warrior is a person who strives to master himself and his situation, a process that normally does not involve the use of physical force. Being a Wiccan and being a Warrior overlap; both have to do with forging your reality into something that you desire. The aim of the Warrior path is "invincibility, victory without battle, and unassailable strength" through better understanding yourself and your situation.[3] The Wiccan Warrior unites the elements of the two paths to form an even more effective harmonious path.

This work belongs to the second generation of Wicca. It steps beyond our beginnings and redefines the practice, ethics, and magick of Wicca. I do this from a Warrior perspective, since accessing the Warrior archetype is one of the most effective ways to give you this control over your life. By combining the archetypes of both the Wiccan (or Magickian) and Warrior we end up with a more effective system than either of the two on their own. This book takes a slightly different approach from most other books on Wicca. It is meant to be a starting point. This book is a guide to help you create your own Wiccan practice and your own Book of Shadows. Any effective Book of Shadows is ultimately a personal journal. In this journal you will record the magick that allows you to make changes in your life. And taking charge of the change in your life is what being a Wiccan and a Warrior is all about. For as the Greek philosopher Heraclitus told us, "Change alone is unchanging."[4]

This work is divided into five books. Each of these books is related to one of the five elements that make up the Wiccan's world. There is one element for each point of the pentagram, which is the symbol of Wicca: Spirit, Air, Fire, Water, and Earth. Each of the five books also relates to one of the sides of the Witch's Pyramid (more on this later).

Note: In this age of gender equality I heartily dislike terms such as s/he. In this work I alternate the use of "he" and "she" in an attempt to achieve a balance.

If you already have a Book of Shadows, this book can be used to personalize it. If you don't, this book will serve as a manual to help you develop your own.

Set out your writing materials and turn to the first blank page. It's time to begin your journey down the path of the Wiccan Warrior.

Endnotes

1. Calvert Watkins, ed. *The American Heritage Dictionary of Indo-European Roots* (Revised). Initial asterisks are a standard linguistic convention indicating a hypothesized word in an extinct language.

2. Judy Harrow. (1993). "Basics for Beginners," *Protean Book of Shadows*, Proteus Coven.

3. Sun Tzu, Thomas Cleary, trans. (1991). *The Art of War*, Preface, p. viii.

4. Heraclitus (c. 535 B.C.E.–475 B.C.E.). *Herakleitos & Diogenes, Pt. 1*, fragment 23 (1976; translated by Guy Davenport).

Book One

THE BOOK OF SPIRIT

OR WICCANS, THERE are five elements that make up the universe: Air, Fire, Water, Earth, and Spirit. It is Spirit that is central, holding the other four elements together. Without Spirit, nothing else is possible.

So that is where we will begin our Warrior journey, with Spirit.

But those rare souls whose spirit gets magically into the hearts of men, leave behind them something more real and warmly personal than bodily presence, an ineffable and eternal thing. It is everlasting life touching us as something more than a vague, recondite concept. The sound of a great name dies like an echo; the splendor of fame fades into nothing; but the grace of a fine spirit pervades the places through which it has passed, like the haunting loveliness of mignonette.

James Thurber, "Collecting Himself"

1

Divinity

All good fortune is a gift of the gods, and . . . you don't win the favor of the ancient gods by being good, but by being bold.

Anita Brookner, "Writers at Work"

"SPIRIT FIRST, TECHNIQUE second." This is the advice that Ginchin Funakoshi, one of the founders of modern Karate, gave to his students in his "20 Rules for the Dojo." To be both a Wiccan and a Warrior, you must take Funakoshi's advice. You must first capture the spirit within you.

Everything in life is made up of energy. Even the things around us that we consider to be "solid" material are just energy; it is our perception of them that makes them seem "solid." We are made up of this same energy. It flows through us. We are connected to the world around us by this energetic link, though as yet few people in our modern society are aware of this connection. In 1982, Alain Aspect and his team of physicists in Paris confirmed such a connection. Physicists now call this phenomenon the "zero-point field." This resonates throughout our reality, allowing energy exchange at a quantum level.

Wiccans are monists. We believe that the divine is imminent in everything around us. We do not separate the divine from the everyday world as the Christians do. "The world is the garment that divinity puts on in order to be seen."[1] Everything around us is divine.

I don't worship. Worshiping implies that the deity being worshiped is separate from us. Worship is part of a dualist worldview common in the Judeo-Christian-Islamic religious systems. It is interesting that people in these systems often accuse others of idolatry. Idolatry is exactly what many Jews, Christians, and Muslims are engaged in. They put deities up on pedestals and bow down to them. An external system. That is what worship is.

The Judeo-Christian-Islamic world view can be summarized by this statement, "God is the potter and the world is the pot." This implies that God is not present in the world. This in turn suggests that it is not possible for humans to be in the presence of the divine.

I repeat: I don't worship. Deities are metaphors, portals, points of access to the divine. I connect with divinity. I am immersed in divinity. I commune with the divine. I entrain with it. It is a part of me already. By writing this work, I do not mean to imply that I am presenting the word of the Goddess or God to you. I don't need to. What I am telling you is that you don't need me to serve as a translator or intermediary for the divine. All you have to do is listen. The Goddess and God will speak to you just as surely as they speak to me.

The archetypes or images of deity that we create to help us comprehend them are as ephemeral as humankind. Wiccans and their deities have a symbiotic relationship; we create one another. We were created from divine energy and it is our energy that creates our concepts of divinity. It is in divinity that we find ourselves. Praying is talking to yourself.

There is an expression we use to one another as a greeting within the Wiccan community, "Thou art God/dess." This is done in recognition of the spark of divinity within each of us. This attitude is not unique to our spiritual path, but it is not the perception prevalent within Western society these days. You have a direct link with the Goddess and the God. They are an energetic part of you. You don't need some clergy person to intercede for you. All Wiccans are clergy. You don't need to contact them through intermediaries of any sort, as Doreen Valiente told us in her beautiful Charge of the Goddess:

> Now listen to the words of the Great Mother, who was of old also called among men Artemis, Astarte, Athene, Dione, Melusine, Aphrodite, Cerridwen, Dana, Arianrhod, Isis, Bride, and by many other names. At her altars, the youth of Lacedaemon in Sparta made due sacrifice.
>
> Whenever ye have need of anything, once in the month, and better it be when the moon is full, then shall ye assemble in some secret place, and adore the spirit of me, who am Queen of all witches.
>
> There shall ye assemble, ye who are fain to learn all sorcery, yet have not yet won its deepest secrets; to these will I teach things that are as yet unknown.
>
> And ye shall be free from slavery; and as a sign that ye be really free, ye shall be naked in your rites; and ye shall dance, sing, feast, make music and love, all in my praise. For mine is the ecstacy of the spirit, and mine also is joy on earth; for my law is love unto all beings.
>
> Keep pure your highest ideal; strive ever towards it, let naught stop you or turn you aside; for mine is the secret door which opens upon the door of youth, and mine is the cup of the wine of life, and the Cauldron of Cerridwen, which is the Holy Grail of immortality.

I am the gracious Goddess, who gives the gift of joy unto the heart of man. Upon earth, I give the knowledge of the spirit eternal; and beyond death, I give peace, and freedom, and reunion with those who have gone before.

Nor do I demand sacrifice; for behold, I am the Mother of all living, and my love is poured out upon the earth.

Hear ye the words of the Star Goddess; she is in the dust of whose feet are the hosts of heaven, whose body encircles the universe.

I am the beauty of the green earth, and the white moon among the stars, and the mystery of the waters, and the desire of the heart of man.

Call unto my soul; arise and come unto me; for I am the soul of nature, who gives life to the universe. From me all things proceed, and unto me all things must return; and before my face, beloved of Gods and of men, let thine innermost divine self be enfolded in the rapture of the infinite.

Let my worship be within the heart that rejoiceth; for behold, all acts of love and pleasure are my rituals. And therefore let there be beauty and strength, power and compassion, honour and humility, mirth and reverence within you.

And thou who thinkest to seek for me, know thy seeking and yearning shall avail thee not unless thou knowest the mystery; that if that which thou seekest thou findest not within thee, thou wilt never find it without thee. For behold, I have been with thee from the beginning; and I am that which is attained at the end of desire.

Open your Book of Shadows and write down this Charge of the Goddess. Make it the prologue of your Book of Shadows. Let it remind you of the divinity within you. You are divine.

I don't worship deity, but I do invoke deity. I call upon divine aspects related to the magick I want to work. In doing so I am empowering those parts of myself that I need to make the magick effective. Invocation is a means of accessing your higher consciousness or your subconscious mind.

To re-establish a connection with the natural world around you is to reconnect with divine energy. Many people in our modern world have lost sight of their connection to the natural world. They are walled up in modern cities of concrete, plastic, and glass with very little of the natural world in sight. Their occupations have nothing to do with nature.

For example, police officers like me spend a great deal of their time dealing with dysfunctional people and criminals. We find these people in seedy tenements, reeking crack houses, and the filthy alleys of major cities. We police officers spend our entire shift immersed in tragedy, danger, and adrenaline. I've known a lot of cops who have lost sight of the fact that there is a beautiful world out there full of normal people. It is easy to see how this happens. Police officers often do not see many positive things in the course of a shift. It takes an effort to put this all away when it is time to go home at the end of the day. Many cops don't ever think to make this effort.

When you lose this connection to nature, you lose respect for the natural world and, ultimately, yourself. It is this connection to nature that people started yearning for at the outset of the Industrial Revolution. People left this connection behind as they flocked to major cities looking for work. This attempt to reconnect to nature is one of the elements that attracts so many people to Wicca these days. To become a Wiccan is to strive to reconnect yourself with this natural energy. Wiccans acknowledge this natural energy by personifying it as the Goddess and her consort the Horned God. Wicca is a nature religion attuned to the cycles of the cosmos. Many people come to Wicca to heal themselves by reintegrating themselves with these cycles.

Unlike Christianity, which is a monotheistic religion (i.e., "one god"), Modern Wicca is ditheistic—we recognize both male and female aspects of divinity. This reflects the two genders that we see all around us in the natural world. Wicca is a fertility religion that recognizes the power in both female and male.

In Wicca, all of the differing Goddesses of the world are seen to be simply aspects of one Goddess. Likewise, all of the Gods of the world are simply aspects of one God. The ultimate divine source is unlimited and eternal. It is hard for humans to handle in this form. Wiccans intentionally limit the forms of divinity that they create in order that they may use them more effectively. These narrower aspects of the Goddess and God are easier to use and visualize in our rites.

It was Apuleius who first described this concept in his book *Metamorphoses*. Apuleius declared Isis, his favorite female deity, to be the embodiment of all other Goddesses. It was also Apuleius who associated the Goddess with the moon and with nature. The idea that there is one Goddess and one God, each with multiple aspects, resurfaced in the literature of the early 1800s. This concept was popularized through the works of poets like Keats, Shelley, and Swinburne and writers like Graves and Joyce. Ultimately it was incorporated into modern Wicca. I don't intend to enter into a lengthy discussion of how this came about in this work. Ronald Hutton's book *Triumph of the Moon* is an excellent resource for anyone wanting to trace the development of modern Paganism.

Many of the world's religions may be classified as "revealed religions." A limited number of prophets claim to have received the word of some deity or other. These prophets claim to receive it either directly or through some messenger or angel (that's what the word angel means: "messenger"). These prophets then dispense this revelation to the masses, usually by passing it on in the form of a holy text of some sort. Then this text is endlessly analyzed and interpreted, applying centuries-old solutions to situations that no longer are applicable. This, in turn, creates immense bureaucracies with all the problems that entails. It was Mark Twain who pointed out to us that "there was never a century nor a country that was short of experts who knew the Deity's mind and were willing to reveal it."[2]

Wicca isn't one of these "revealed" religions. In Wicca, everyone has direct access to deity, making such scripture and structure redundant. Martin Luther started a revolution within the Christian church when he suggested this in his Ninety-Five Theses, which he fastened to the door of All Saints Church in Wittenberg under a full moon on October 31, 1517. This is a major revision in the way religion has been practiced by the majority of Western society in the past few centuries. Every time I see a Wiccan group attempting to use its Book of Shadows as "scripture" I am reminded of this. In this book I'm not going to tell you what I think the Goddess or God has told me to tell you. I'm going to teach you to listen, so that They can tell you Themselves. You have a personal connection to the divine already. All you need to do to access it is to realize it. It will all be revealed to you personally in time.

The Gods won't necessarily speak to you in words. Their lessons arrive in all sorts of ways. Some are rather dramatic, others less so. It could be coming across a lesson that you needed in some book. It could be a timely note from a fellow Warrior. It could be some natural event. I remember calling upon Herne at a midnight solitary Circle beside a huge waterfall in a provincial park many years ago. I almost immediately felt his presence—my hair raising, an inner feeling verging on panic. But I wasn't as good at listening then. I was an inexperienced and impatient young Wiccan and I wasn't paying attention to this presence. I asked Herne for a sign even though I already had received one. Immediately a coyote just outside the Circle behind me howled. As I spun around, the coyote calmly padded off into the woods. Call it a wake-up call. I had my sign.

There is a tendency amongst the followers of various religions of the world to call upon their Gods to sort out their problems for them. They tend to treat deities like some genie out of a bottle that will grant them their wishes if only they ask the right way. Many people fall down on their knees and try to get the Gods to take responsibility for their human failures (that "worship thing" again).

Wicca is not one of these religions. Wiccan author Scott Cunningham once pointed out:

> This is a stalling maneuver, an avoidance of dealing with the bumps on the road of life. However, as Wiccans we can call on the Goddess and God to clear our minds and help us help ourselves.[3]

The Charge of the Goddess tells us that the Goddess and her Consort the Horned God are teachers, advisors, and counselors. More importantly, the Charge tells us that the Gods are within us. They have been from the beginning. This is one of the reasons that I encouraged you to start your spiritual journey with the spirit within yourself. That is where you will find the Goddess and the God—in your heart and soul. The Charge of the Goddess tells us that the Gods are willing to teach you personally. Take their lessons and apply them to your life. Wiccans are responsible for the problems that they encounter on their path through life. You won't be able to overcome these impediments until you accept this responsibility.

In Judeo-Christian-Islamic beliefs God tends to be a fixed element. This isn't the case in Wicca. Wiccans use whatever aspect of deity best suits their purposes. After all, they are all aspects of one universal concept. Different types of magick call for different aspects of deity. As with the ancient Celts, whose deities were very localized, the identity of Wiccan deities varies from one Coven to the next. The deities used by Wiccans are borrowed from mythological systems all over the world. To the outside observer it may seem that the modern Wiccan uses many different deities, not just two. It is a natural assumption, given that the followers of many ancient Pagan religions were polytheistic (i.e., worshipper of many

Gods). While some of these were organized into "family" group-ings like the Gods of Olympus, many were unrelated and were believed to have very narrow spheres of influence.

One of your first tasks as a Wiccan and a Warrior is to chose which aspects of deity you wish to work with. This may change over the years as your circumstances change. I am not going to rec-ommend any particular deity to you. You must make up your own mind what forms of deity and mythology to work with. Your expe-rience and heritage will make some aspects more accessible to you than others. Choosing an aspect of deity that represents the mag-ickal work you intend to carry out helps to energize the magick.

For example, I have a Celtic heritage, so this is the mythology that I use most often in my Wiccan practice. In my youth, however, my parents exposed me to a lot of the Greek classics, as they con-sidered this an important part of my education. As a result, it was deities from Greek mythology that I used in my early Wiccan days. I still have a very strong connection to them. You should experi-ment and find the system that works best for you. Some people feel more comfortable dealing with a Goddess and God who have no names. Others need to use very specific names and forms for the Gods. Use whatever system seems most comfortable to you. These deities are images that speak to your subconscious and they will be most effective if they are familiar symbols (more on this later).

One of the common themes in the literature of the last few decades is that all Mother Goddesses of the ancient world were large, friendly Goddesses of the Earth's fertility. They are pre-sented as benevolent figures like the Catholic Virgin Mary. On the other hand, the dark Goddesses, such as the Morrighan in Celtic mythology or Kali in the Hindu pantheon, are often viewed by people today as terrible Goddesses of death and destruction. Nei-ther of these views is entirely accurate. The problem with both of these interpretations is that neither takes into account the totality of the Goddess.

The Goddess represents the feminine aspect of the balance of forces in nature. Like humans, she has her "light" and "dark" sides. One finds these dual aspects of the Goddess in many mythological systems. For example, in Celtic mythology, the most common duality is the pairing of aspects of war or destruction with aspects of fertility and sex. This may seem confusing or contradictory to a person in Western society today. Yet such Goddesses are the keepers of the doorways between our world and the Otherworld. They open the doors between life and death. They take life and they create it. They give life with the promise of death. A popular Wiccan song reminds us that we all come from the Goddess, and to her we all return. Death comes from life and life from death. We live because we consume dead plants and animals. Thus the Morrighan was a Goddess of both love and death, appearing in myth as both a seductive but deadly maiden and a screaming hag, who takes in order to give.

Another dual aspect is that of the mother and son. For example: In Britain this took the form of Modron (which simply means "mother") and her son Mabon ("son"). Unlike the Christian model of the Virgin Mary and the Christ child, the Celtic Mother Goddess is a dark, mysterious, severe, initiatory figure. Other than this there are quite a few parallels between Christ and Mabon:

- ◆ Both are youthful sons of light
- ◆ Both are mediators between man and the supernatural
- ◆ Both had a virgin birth
- ◆ Both were persecuted as a child by a corrupt king
- ◆ Both had powers of prophecy
- ◆ Both were tempted by great powers
- ◆ Both died a ritual death

One finds many dual aspects in male deities as well. In many mythological systems, one finds recurring themes of a God of

Light battling with a God of Darkness. This is a common theme at Wiccan Yule rituals: the struggle of the Holly and Oak kings. Another example, in the Celtic system, is the bright son Mabon who is balanced by the dark son, represented by hunting Gods such as Cernunnos, lord of animals.

This should not be confused with the Zoroastrian concept of forces of light versus forces of darkness. This is not the concept of Christ versus Antichrist, that was adopted by the Christians and later gave rise to the myths of Yahweh and Satan. The deities Wiccans recognize have twin aspects: dark and light aspects of one deity. The polarities of the male divine are of positive and negative, summer and winter, with each having its own inherent positive and negative qualities. The dark half of the year succeeds the light half of the year, which in turn succeeds the dark half and so on ad infinitum. Whereas the Christian system has one side triumphing over the other, the Wiccan system has positive and negative forces in balance. The Holly King triumphs over the Oak King one season, only to lose to him again a half year later. This cycle repeats endlessly. Wicca is a reflection of the polarity of life and the cycles of the seasons, of the positive and negative qualities inherent in each of us.

The dualities of both the Dark Mother and Son of Light and of the Dark Son versus the Light Son reflect the giving and taking that are both vital parts of the cycle of life. All things end so that new things may begin.

One finds many triple aspects of deities too. Robert Graves created one of the most enduring modern triplicities of the Goddess in Wicca: Maiden, Mother, and Crone. Other trinities that we can identify are:

◆ Destroyer, Beginner, Increaser

Or

◆ Death, Birth, Fruitfulness

Or even

◆ Death, Fertility, Virginity

Male divinity can also be seen in triple aspects. The typical triple pattern for Wiccan Gods is:

◆ Wise Elder
◆ Lord of Animals or Lord of Healing (light and dark aspects of one another)
◆ Bright Youth

In modern Western society people have come to equate beauty with youth. People go to amazing lengths to maintain a youthful appearance, employing makeup, hair dyes, and cosmetic surgery. This is a fixation on the Maiden or Bright Youth aspect. Many people in modern Western society tend to consider pregnant women or old women ugly. Wiccans recognize that beauty takes many forms and that each of the three aspects is beautiful in its season. Aging is not a process to fear. It is simply part of the cycle of life. The Crone and Wise Elder are the keepers of knowledge. We are a reflection of these aspects of deity.

These dualities and triplicities mirror human existence. We are a reflection of divinity and divinity is a reflection of us. In myth we can find lessons to apply to our own situation in life.

Scott Cunningham told us that:

> Discovering the deities of Wicca is a never-ending experience. They constantly reveal themselves. As the shamans say, "Be attentive." All nature is singing to us of Her secrets. The Goddess constantly draws aside Her veil; The God lights us up with inspiration and illumination. We simply don't notice.[4]

Unless we make an effort to. Unless we listen.

Endnotes

1. Phyllis Curott. (14 October 2000). "Exploding Wiccan Dogma," lecture at Blessed Be and Merry Meet in D.C. (BBMMDC) conference in Washington D.C.

2. Mark Twain. (1973). "As Concerns Interpreting the Deity" (1905; repr. in *What Is Man?*, ed. by Paul Baender, 1973).

3. Scott Cunningham. (1989). *Wicca: A Guide for the Solitary Practitioner*, p. 13.

4. Ibid., p. 17.

2

The Wiccan Rede

*Why don't you take a good look at yourself and describe
what you see?*
  Baby, baby, baby, do you like it?

Robert Plant, Jimmy Page, and John Paul Jones,
"Misty Mountain Hop"

THE FOUNDATION OF the Wiccan Warrior's spirit is the Wiccan
Rede. The Wiccan Rede is a plan of action for the Wiccan Warrior. It advises you how to conduct yourself on the Warrior's
path. The Wiccan Rede is deceptively simple. Like many simple
rules, however, a lot of things flow from it.

The Wiccan Rede

An It Harm None, Do What Thou Wilt.

Let the Wiccan Rede be the first entry after the Charge of the
Goddess in your Book of Shadows. Give it a page to itself. Make it
a title page if you like. The Wiccan Rede deserves special promi-
nence. This is your starting point on the Wiccan Warrior's path.

A Wiccan cannot call themselves a Wiccan or a Warrior if they do not adhere to the Wiccan Rede.

In my previous book, *Wiccan Warrior,* I made the point that the Wiccan Rede was a very Warrior-oriented approach to life. The Wiccan Rede requires Wiccans to use their heads instead of someone else's list of rules. It requires us to take responsibility for our actions rather than relinquishing it to someone or something else.

Wicca is not a Zoroastrian system, like Christianity, having only extremes of light versus dark, good versus evil, right versus wrong. That sort of system is an approach that requires no thought. There are no shades of gray. It is composed of long lists of rules and rigid codes. Robin Wood pointed out in her book *When, Why . . . If*:

> There are no gray areas here, no moral dilemmas, just right and wrong, simple and clear cut. There are no natural consequences for your actions, no personal responsibility for any outcome, no reasoning, no thinking of any kind required; in short no ethics at all, just a list of things to be memorized, and a simple formula of repentance and forgiveness if you forget or decide to skip one.[1]

The Wiccan Rede is not a rule. It is a statement counseling us to think. Personal responsibility is the basis of the Wiccan ethical system. We must take responsibility for our actions and think about what we are doing. Rules are for training young children to be adults. At some point you must grow up and understand the reasons for the rules. This understanding should replace the rules. Wiccans don't steal because it is illegal; Wiccans don't steal because Wiccans understand that stealing is wrong.

Is it really possible to make it through life without harming someone or something? We eat to stay alive. We eat things that were alive. The death of living things brings us life. To survive cancer we must kill cancer cells. In India the sect of Jains attempts to adhere to a very strict principle of harming none. They wear masks so that they don't accidentally inhale a bug. They wear bells to warn insects of their approach. They don't pick an apple from a tree, they wait for it to fall. But, no matter how hard they try, they are bound to have an adverse affect on something in the world around them. Their presence affects everything around them.

I'm not suggesting that you should go about in a mask and bells. I'm not telling you to starve yourself. I'm asking you to treat everything around you as divine. To realize that everything around you is worthy of respect. Wiccan priestesses Ashleen O'Gaea and Carol Garr put it this way: "When something dies so that we can continue to live, it's important to recognize that contribution, and to respect it, and honor the creature that makes it."[2] If you believe that everything in the universe is divine, then violence will be contrary to your nature. You are less likely to harm someone or something that you respect.

Some people have challenged me to explain how I reconcile my job as a police officer (or as some people have put it, an agent of the state) and the Wiccan Rede. Let me give you two examples. First, let's say I see a young woman working as a prostitute on a street corner. This activity is illegal. The law authorizes me to go over and arrest her for engaging in such activity. I don't have to think about it. It is illegal, so I arrest her.

But suppose I went over first and spoke to this young woman. Suppose I asked her why she was there on that street corner prostituting herself. She tells me that her mother's fifth husband threw her out of the house. She is too young to collect welfare and has no job skills. This is the only option that she thinks that she has. I have the power to arrest her, but will arresting her solve her problem? Won't she just go right back out again when she is released and do it again? How else is she going to feed herself? What choices does she have?

Do you see what I'm getting at? The Rede asks us to examine our actions carefully. It advises us to use our heads and solve the problem, rather than taking the easy way out. If I solve the problem, then hopefully she won't be back on the street. So I find social service agencies and resources to help her overcome this problem. I have many powers of arrest, but I use my common sense before I decide to apply them. This is how I apply the Rede to my police profession.

I sometimes have to use force to control the violence of others. I'm not violent in this situation. It isn't my karma if some perpetrator starts a fight: It is his. I become his "karma accelerator" by intervening to control him.

The first half of the Wiccan Rede requires the Warrior to avoid violence. The misconception that violence is a part of the Warrior's path is a common one in today's society. Words like "war," "combat," or "fight" are the kind of words that pop into the average person's head when they hear the word "Warrior." I assure you that if you give in to violence and anger, you are connecting yourself to the shadow side of the Warrior. Ultimately hatred is a projection of your own shadow. If you hate someone or something, it is actually yourself that you hate. This is one of the reasons that many serious martial artists are ultimately less aggressive than they may have been before they commenced their studies. Martial arts is essentially a study of oneself. True Warriors are at peace with themselves because they know themselves. They have nothing to prove to anyone anymore. Traditional martial arts schools are as much a seminary, where one studies philosophy, as a practice floor where one learns the application of physical force. It is the philosophy that acts as a check and balance to the physical part of the art.

Being a Warrior is not about violence. A true Warrior wins most of his battles with his head, not his hands. The idea that nonviolence is an integral part of the Warrior's path is a very old one. We can find examples of this concept in all places and ages. Let's look at some examples.

- In the fifth century B.C.E., the Greek historian Herodotus said that "where wisdom is called for, force is of little use."

- A century later, the Chinese Warrior philosopher Sun Tzu told us: "Those who win every battle are not really skillful—those who render others' armies helpless without fighting are the best of all."[3]

- In the final ritual of the Masai manhood ritual, the senior tribal elders encourage the graduates to "drop your weapons and use your head and wisdom instead."[4]

- In the sixteenth century C.E. the Samurai philosopher Miyamoto Musashi told us that the "trained martial artist . . . truly acts only in response to aggression. He does not seek it out. When made, his responses are nonresistant and nonviolent. He is a man of peace."[5]

Consider these statements carefully. Note them down in your Book of Shadows. Keep them in mind whenever you are considering the use of force.

The second half of the Wiccan rede seems equally simple: Do what thou wilt. In modern English: Do what you will. What is your will? Do you know what you want from life? Or are you trying to conform to someone else's expectations? What direction are you going in your life? Do you have specific objectives and goals to achieve?

Generations of men in my family have been in the military. My father was a flight engineer in the Canadian Royal Air Force. He wanted me to become an air force pilot. More than this, my father wanted me to become an officer and a gentleman, since he came from a working-class family. For a long time I pursued his dream, thinking that it was my own. When I became a Wiccan I began to examine this in light of the Wiccan Rede. Ultimately I gave up a military path to pursue a career in law enforcement. This was my dream.

Be careful with this, however. "Do what thou wilt" is only half of the Rede. This is not the same thing as Aleister Crowley's well-known line (borrowed from the author Rabelais,[6] who in turn borrowed it from St. Augustine):[7]

> *"Do what thou wilt shall be the whole of the law."*[8]

Rebellion is often a useful instrument of change, as it was for me in this instance. Yet simply rebelling and doing the opposite of whatever family or society seems to want for you is not the Warrior's way. The Warrior is not just a rebel. The Warrior tempers his actions with the responsibility implied by the first half of the Rede. The malcontent has no boundaries. Malcontents perceive others (e.g., the authorities or his family) as the problem and simply choose to oppose them. Such people raise and use energy only for themselves. To accept freedom without responsibility is to turn hedonism into religion. The rebel is the shadow side of the Warrior.

I have encountered some people who profess to be Wiccan who seem to interpret the Wiccan Rede to mean: "Do whatever feels good." Perhaps they are thinking of Crowley's "Do what thou wilt . . ." Hedonism is an attitude that the Wiccan Warrior cannot afford to indulge in. A Wiccan Warrior cannot afford to be so self-centered. You cannot embrace freedom without any consideration for how your actions will affect others. If you want to be a Warrior, you must accept responsibility for yourself. You have to carefully consider how your actions and appearance reflect on yourself and your community.

The moment that I became a police officer, I put myself under a spotlight of public scrutiny. The moment that I became public about being a Wiccan, this scrutiny intensified. After all, people have been bombarded with propaganda about Witches being Satanists for years. So it was only natural to expect my police department and the public to examine me closely and at length to see if I was really some dangerous Satanic cult member. The greater the responsibility attached to your profession, the greater the likelihood that scrutiny of this sort will be turned in your direction.

In my case, I knew that the only way that these people could reassure themselves was to allow them to investigate me. Unfortunately for me, this process of investigation went on for years. One of the reasons for this is that the investigators were turning up not only propaganda about Satanism, but also media accounts of bizarre behavior by certain members of the Wiccan community. Naturally this behavior reflected on both myself and the rest of the Wiccan community.

As a Wiccan Warrior who is public about his beliefs, I accept this scrutiny. Playwright George Bernard Shaw once said, "Liberty means responsibility. That is why most men dread it."[9] A Warrior must be impeccable. To earn respect you must make yourself respectable. This has meant a certain amount of sacrifice for me. I suppose I could easily have felt sorry for myself for being subjected to such scrutiny and attention. I could have called such treatment unfair and unjust. Others in my place might have felt themselves to be at the mercy of the fates, or would have felt this way if they did not take responsibility for their actions as a Warrior should. Life is a challenge and I treat it as such. I don't seek pain and frustration. But if they come, a Warrior puts them to use.

In the end I prevailed because of taking this position. I didn't give my employer anything to use against me. The authorities gave up on their surveillance of me as they found nothing to justify continuing it. One way or another, they eventually came to respect me and my beliefs.

The Warrior accepts boundaries. He knows how far he can go and will go no further. These boundaries may change with time and changes in circumstances and abilities, but they are clearly defined. Warriors identify the true nature of their problems and take responsibility for their solution. The Wiccan Warrior's thoughts go to the community. It is for the community that the Wiccan Warrior raises energy. This is what the Wiccan Rede is all about. Of course this course of action will benefit the Wiccan Warrior as well.

While the last half of the Wiccan Rede encourages you to follow your bliss, the first half of the Rede calls upon Wiccans and Warriors to take responsibility for their actions. That's the catch. The Wiccan Rede tells us to temper our freedom with self-discipline. This is exactly what the Wiccan Rede is telling us. A person who seeks freedom without any responsibility is a rebel, not a Warrior or a Wiccan. Complete freedom of will is an illusion in any case. "The will is never free," Joyce Cary once wrote, "It is always attached to an object, a purpose. It is simply the engine in the car—it can't steer."[10]

Wiccan priestess and author Amber K put the matter of personal responsibility very eloquently:

> You begin by taking responsibility for your life and everything in it. This is part of coming into your power. You cannot be a victim, the pawn of others' schemes and the plaything of fate, and be a magician too. Accustom yourself to the idea that everything in your life—every event, relationship, thought and material object—is there because you chose it."[11]

Most of the events in our lives are not random. Things happen to us either because we have created this reality we live in, or because it is time for us to learn a lesson from this particular event. There is an old magickal adage: Be careful what you ask for, because you'll get it.

If you want to be taken seriously by society, you must take yourself seriously. Bob Dylan described a hero as "someone who understands the degree of responsibility that comes with his freedom."[12] Your actions as well as your appearance send a message to the world around you. The Warrior keeps this in mind and uses his actions and appearance to communicate a specific message. If you don't like the way that you are being treated by the people around you, take a look at yourself. You may be the object of discrimination, but it is just possible that it is something that you are doing that is attracting this negative reaction.

There is an old saying: "Choice, not chance, determines destiny."[13] Many people let the winds of change blow them hither and thither through life. Abandoning yourself to "fate" in this manner is not the Warrior's way. The Wiccan Warrior needs to actively participate in life. There will always be some variables in life over which you have no control. The Warrior does not let these variables dictate his path through life. Warriors identify those variables over which they do have control and use them to their best advantage. Warriors take charge of their lives. The Wiccan Warrior's life is self-made.

You make up for the things that you can't influence with the things that you can control. "We cannot direct the wind, but we can adjust our sails."[14] What you are is what you've made yourself into. Where you are is where you've been. If you aren't what you want to be, it is up to you to do something about it. It is as simple as that. Change won't happen until you change. I strive to create my life spontaneously rather than letting it be determined by my past, using the principles and magickal techniques of Wicca. What I am is what I've forged with the energy I've raised and the magick that I've worked. I cause change in conformity with my will.

So the next thing that I'm going to ask you to do on this Warrior's path is to dedicate yourself to being responsible for yourself. You're going to take a good look at yourself and your situation and decide to achieve self-mastery. You can't master magick (or anything else) until your master yourself. To be a Warrior, you must make this one of your most important goals in life.

This leads us to my definition of a Warrior. Make a note of this in your Book of Shadows:

Definition of a Warrior

A Warrior is a person who makes a fearless and objective inventory of his or her personal characteristics and then uses this information to take control of his or her life.

A Warrior must develop an understanding of her talents and limitations. A Warrior then achieves her goals using a combination of this self-awareness and her will to overcome weaknesses, fears, and limitations. The Wiccan Warrior's path is the Wiccan Rede in action. It is taking responsibility for your actions. It has nothing to do with being a police officer or serving in the military. It has nothing to do with being male or female. It is commitment to the process of taking charge of your life.

I've listed a number of Warrior Precepts in this work for you to include in your Book of Shadows. I have borrowed the first Warrior precept from an inscription dating from the sixth century B.C.E. at the Oracle of Apollo at Delphi:

First Warrior Precept

Know Thyself.

Sun Tzu once said "that when you know yourself and others, victory is not in danger; when you know sky and earth, victory is inexhaustible."[15] The first Warrior precept tells us that to have control of ourselves we must develop self-knowledge. To know yourself is to develop a personal inventory of all the skills that you possess, as well as those you will require. It is a matter of making an honest appraisal of yourself, listing your strong and weak points objectively and truthfully. Knowledge of self is the basis that you will work from as a Wiccan Warrior. This is why I have emphasized self-examination in this chapter. For "the one self-knowledge worth having is to know one's mind."[16]

Keeping this definition in mind, I want you to write the following dedication on the page following the Wiccan Rede at the beginning of your Book of Shadows:

Dedication

I vow that I will conduct a fearless and objective self-inventory of my characteristics. I commit myself to use this knowledge for personal growth leading to self-mastery.

Note: At some point you may wish to do some sort of initiatory ritual or ceremony to dedicate formally yourself to the Warrior's path. For now it is sufficient to take this vow.

Turn to a new page in your Book of Shadows. The title of this page is the first of the Warrior Precepts: *Know Thyself.* Under this heading take the time to list as many of the characteristics that make up your personality as you can. Later you can come back and add to the list or modify it. Be objective. This list won't be of any use to you at all if you are not honest with yourself. This is your personal journal, and no one else need see it.

This list is your personal toolkit. You are going to use the information on your list to transform your life. Every characteristic on this list will be useful to you at some time or other. Note that I am using the term "characteristics" here rather than a phrase like "strengths and weaknesses." In a given circumstance any one of your characteristics could be either. For example, a stubborn nature can be a hindrance in certain circumstances. Yet, in another set of circumstances, stubbornness may be exactly the characteristic you need to use to push on through obstacles to achieve your objective. The trick is learning how to use or modify these characteristics in accordance with the Wiccan Rede and apply them to your situation.

So far you have learned the definition of a Warrior and the Wiccan Rede. You have learned the first Warrior Precept: *Know Thyself.* You've have done some serious soul-searching and have come up with a personal inventory that you can use to achieve self-mastery. Next we will examine a concept that will help us make our magick more effective, the Witch's Pyramid.

Endnotes

1. Robin Wood. (1996). *When, Why . . . If,* Introduction, p. ii.

2. Ashleen O'Gaea and Carol Garr. (2000). *Circles Behind Bars: A Complete Handbook for the Incarcerated Witch,* unpublished.

3. Sun Tzu (Thomas Cleary, trans.). (1991). *The Art of War,* p. 18.

4. Carol Beckwith and Angela Fisher. (Sept. 1999). "Masai Passage to Manhood," *National Geographic* magazine, Vol. 196, No. 3, p. 65.

5. Miyamoto Musashi. (1988). *The Book of Five Rings,* Introduction, p. xxvii.

6. François Rabelais. *Gargantua and Pantagruel,* Book 1, Chapter 57. Rabelais dropped Augustine's "Love God" part and simply put "Do what you will" over the gateway of Friar John's fantasy of the perfect monastery. He intended this as a plug for his own vision of the ideal libertine lifestyle.

7. St. Augustine. Augustine wrote, "Love God and do what you will." He was promoting a shift from the classical Pagan emphasis on religious practice and duty to the new Christian emphasis on uniformity of belief.

8. Aleister Crowley. *Magick in Theory and Practice,* Introduction, p. xxii.

9. George Bernard Shaw. (1856–1950). *Man and Superman,* "Maxims for Revolutionists: Liberty and Equality."

10. Joyce Cary. (1957). Interview in *Writers at Work* (First Series, ed. by Malcolm Cowley, 1958).

11. Amber K. (1990). *True Magick: A Beginner's Guide,* p. 65.

12. Bob Dylan. (1985). Interview in booklet accompanying the *Biograph* album set.

13. Author unknown, Weight Watchers book.

14. Ibid.

15. Sun Tzu (Thomas Cleary, trans.). (1991). *The Art of War,* p. 87.

16. F. H. Bradley. (1930). *Aphorisms,* no. 8.

3

The Witch's Pyramid

The Magus, the Theurgist, the True Witch stand on a pyramid of power whose foundation is a profound knowledge of the occult, whose four sides are creative imagination, a will of steel, a living faith and the ability to keep silent.

Clifford Bias, *The Ritual Book of Magic*

THE WITCH'S PYRAMID is a concept that I briefly discussed in my first book, *Wiccan Warrior*. It was first proposed by Clifford Bias in *The Ritual Book of Magic* and expanded upon in Amber K's *True Magic*. It is a five-sided model that helps us understand the interaction of five important magickal principles:

To Know, To Keep Silent, To Dare, To Imagine, To Will.

These five principles or axioms are the cornerstones of the magick of the Wiccan Warrior. Each of these axioms interact together to form a functioning whole. Imagine that each of these five principles forms a side of a pyramid. If any one of them is missing or flawed, the magickal energy enclosed within this pyramid will escape and the resulting magick will be ineffective. The Wiccan Warrior hones his Witch's Pyramid to seal up these flaws. At the same time, he seals up the flaws in his own character.

To Know

The principle of the Witch's Pyramid that we are dealing with in this Book of Spirit is *To Know*. This principle represents the base of this Pyramid. I have intentionally labeled this principle "to know" rather than "knowledge." Knowing is more than accumulating pieces of knowledge. Knowing is awareness. It is a dynamic process. As Dan Millman once said: "Understanding is one-dimensional . . . Realization, on the other hand, is three-dimensional."[1] Another word for this process is "gnosis," a Greek word meaning "knowing" on a deep psychological and spiritual level.

Poet e.e. cummings once described knowledge as "a polite word for dead but not buried imagination."[2] This is a very apt description, since knowing is a process directly linked to an active awareness of the world around you. Knowing links knowledge with awareness.

Those who have read Robert Heinlein's *Stranger in a Strange Land* will be familiar with the term "grok." Grok is a term which he invented to describe the process of coming to a complete and full understanding and awareness of a thing in real time. Or, as Heinlein described it, "to understand so thoroughly that the observer becomes part of the observed . . ."[3] This is what I mean by my use of the term "knowing." The Wiccan Warrior places himself in the moment and experiences it fully. This experiencing brings understanding.

When the average person examines something they tend to immobilize it. They tend to isolate the thing from its environment. Knowing is perceiving without this immobilization. Bruce Lee once said: "Knowledge is fixed in time, whereas, knowing is continual. Knowledge comes from a source, from an accumulation, from a conclusion, while knowing is movement."[4] It is this characteristic which links this axiom with one of the other five: *To Keep Silent* (which we will discuss in chapter 8).

It is knowing that allows the Warrior to avoid the use of violence. In the eighteenth century, English author Samuel Johnson told us, "Man is not weak; knowledge is more than equivalent to force."[5] This principle is the basis of many martial arts like Aikido. Being a Warrior is not so much a matter of using force as it is using the force of your opponents against themselves.

Now it is time to write down the second Warrior precept in your Book of Shadows:

Second Warrior Precept

Nurture the ability to perceive the truth in all matters.

Perception is a tricky business; things aren't always the way that they seem on the surface. Psychologists Robert Moore and Douglas Gillette described knowing as a personal "'bullshit detector;' it sees through denial and exercises discernment."[6] The Warrior must learn to see through deception and illusion to grasp the true nature of her situation. The Wiccan Warrior must learn to dip below the surface and arrive at a true understanding of things in order to act appropriately and effectively.

The only way to control something is to understand it. The more you know about something, the more control you have over it. Knowledge is power. Magick is knowing. There is an old Japanese saying: "From one thing know ten thousand things." The Warrior uses knowing to take charge of his life. Knowing is the foundation from which accurate perception stems. From this foundation the Warrior can separate what is real from what is illusion.

This leads us to the third Warrior precept for you to enter in your Book of Shadows:

Third Warrior Precept

You create your own reality.

This is the goal that you are going to use this "knowing" for. This the ultimate purpose of magick. The second half of the Wiccan Rede encourages us to do just this: Do what thou wilt. It invites us to go forward and be what we want to be. The Wiccan Rede encourages us to throw off our chains and follow our bliss. Once you set yourself free, you can accomplish anything. It is this aspect of knowing that links it to one of the other sides of the Witch's Pyramid: *To Dare* (which we will discuss in chapter 12). I'm not asking you to change into someone else. I'm telling you that by accessing Warrior energy you can become something more.

In this chapter you have learned two Warrior Precepts: (1) *Nurture the ability to perceive the truth in all matters,* and (2) *You create your own reality.* You've learned about the Witch's Pyramid. You've discovered that the base of the Witch's Pyramid is knowing. In the next chapter we will see how the concepts of karma and honor fit into our developing understanding of the Warrior's path.

Endnotes

1. Dan Millman. *The Way of the Peaceful Warrior,* p. 26.
2. e.e. cummings. (1951). "Jotting," *Wake,* no. 10.
3. Robert A. Heinlein. (1987). *Stranger in a Strange Land,* p. 271.
4. Bruce Lee. (1975). *Tao of Jeet Kune Do,* p. 16.
5. Samuel Johnson. (1759). *The History of Rasselas,* ch. 13.
6. Robert Moore and Douglas Gillette. (1990). *King, Warrior, Magician, Lover: Rediscovering the Archetypes of the Mature Masculine,* p. 100.

4

Honor, Karma, and the Law of Three-Fold Return

In this world a man must either be an anvil or a hammer.

Henry Wadsworth Longfellow
Hyperion, "The Story of Brother Berdardus"

IN WESTERN SOCIETY there is a romantic notion that there was an code of chivalry by which the medieval knights lived. With this in mind, many people have commented on the strong influence of the works of Asian martial artists and philosophers that I incorporated into my previous book, *Wiccan Warrior.* These people asked me why I had not included more of a Western perspective on Warrior philosophy. Where was the Medieval Code of Chivalry?

The answer is quite simple. Medieval chivalry is a myth. In the West there was no standard set of duties and ideals, commonly called chivalry. The concept of chivalry changed constantly throughout the Middle Ages in order to keep up with changing socio-economic realities. The most common characteristic of the Hundred Years War wasn't chivalry, it was the *chevauchée.* Chevauchée is a French term applied to a tactic more commonly referred to as "scorched earth" nowadays. Knights would lead their armies across the countryside, plundering and pillaging whatever they needed to provision themselves and burning everything else. There was little chivalry involved in this procedure.

Chivalry in the Middle Ages was a romantic legend. If you study the works of medieval scholars like Chrétien de Troyes, Ramon Lull, Geoffrey de Charny, and Honoret Bonet, you can identify a number of common themes. In his modern Code of Chivalry, Brian Price lists these common themes: prowess, justice, loyalty, defense, courage, faith, humility, largesse, and nobility.[1] These are all admirable virtues. In other words, the ideal of chivalry is that the Warrior must act in an responsible and honorable fashion. Such ideals may have been largely a romantic legend in the past. Even the Warrior's Code of Bushido in Japan was a set of ideals that many did not live up to in real life. This shouldn't hold you back. There is no reason why the modern Wiccan Warrior cannot adopt such codes of conduct and make them as a reality in his life.

One way of doing so is to incorporate the fourth Warrior Precept into your life. Write this precept in your Book of Shadows:

Fourth Warrior Precept

Develop a sense of right action.

Webster's New Twentieth Century Dictionary defines honor as "a sense of what is right, just and true; dignified respect for character, springing from probity, principle, or moral rectitude." This is what I call right action. Simply stated, right action is "what is right, just, and true."

The Wiccan Warrior must develop a fine sense of "right action." Right Action is what Robin Wood describes as finding the balance point: "The spot where all the possible outcomes on one side of a decision are weighed against all the possible outcomes on the other side, and they come out even."[2] Grace and guilt do not exist. The Wiccan Warrior replaces guilt with responsibility and honor. Right action is having a sense of impartial justice. A Warrior must put aside bias and favoritism. The Wiccan Rede reminds us that what is right for you must also be right for others.

The 79th and 80th Ordains in the Gardnerian system of Wicca read, "Ever remember, ye are the ' . . . Children of the Goddess,' so never do anything to disgrace them or her." In plain terms: Never boast, never threaten, never say you would wish ill of anyone. These Ordains clearly call upon Wiccans on the Warrior's path to heed the Warrior Precept of Right Action. They remind us to honor the Wiccan Rede. If the Wiccan Warrior does something that adversely affects another, she does something to make it right to the person affected.

Of course, no reparations or apologies are necessary if one avoids behavior that might harm another. There is no room for sinister designs in your heart if you believe in "Right Action." Right Action and responsibility go hand in hand. Let Right Action govern your behavior towards others. Abigail Van Buren once said, "The best index to a person's character is (*a*) how he treats people who can't do him any good, and (*b*) how he treats people who can't fight back."[3] Respect is something that you earn. To earn respect you must give respect. As I pointed out earlier, everything around you is divine and thus worthy of respect.

There are many ways of giving respect. Here are some examples that relate to those mythical codes of Chivalry and Bushido:

◆ A Wiccan Warrior's word is his bond. A Wiccan Warrior strives to be known for his commitment. Keep your word and you will win the loyalty of others. Respect is something that you earn.

◆ Be generous in so far as your resources allow. Charity is a virtue.

◆ Do not waste other people's valuable time by being late. I wince every time I hear tardy people excusing themselves by saying that they are on "Pagan Standard Time." This is an ignorant expression that clearly demonstrates how little the person using it respects you.

◆ There is a modern Masonic saying: "Engage in acts of random kindness and senseless beauty." This is a way of leading by example. If you want the world to be a wonderful place, do wonderful things.

Karma and the Law of Three-Fold Return

In Judeo-Christian-Islamic systems, transgressors are threatened with divine retribution. They tell you that some deity will whack you if you get out of line.

In Wicca, as in Eastern philosophies, one encounters the concept of karma. The word *karma* derives from a Sanskrit word meaning "action."[4] Karma may be defined as the totality of a person's actions determining their fate in this life or in other incarnations in the future. In other words, karma is the law of cause and effect. The most common Wiccan equivalent of this principle is the Law of Three-Fold Return, established by Raymond Buckland:

"Everything you do comes back to you three times."

Basically this law tells us that we get back three times whatever we put into life. If you do positive works, you will get more abundant positive benefit in return. If you do negative and destructive things to another, then you suffer even worse consequences to yourself. The trouble with this law is that it is describing what in modern terms would be called a "feedback loop." If magickians had come up with proof of this system in the past few centuries, you can be sure that you'd have heard about it. Actually it started as a public relations sound byte to help the public understand that we were harmless Wiccans, not destructive Satanic cult members. It was simple and effective. Actually Gardner's original version was a "two-fold" law. It was in a later press interview that Buckland upped the ante to make it a three-fold law instead. The three-fold version stuck.

I think that it would be more accurate to use the concept of karma rather than the three-fold law to describe what happens in the real world. What you do gets passed forward by others and will eventually make its way back to you. This is another reason that the Wiccan Warrior's path must be a nonviolent one. As Sir Arthur Conan Doyle once put it, "Violence does, in truth, recoil upon the violent, and the schemer falls into the pit which he digs for another."[5] This is why I emphasize the precept of Right Action rather than the Three-Fold Law.

There is an old saying in Wicca: "In order to heal you have to be able to hex." It is interesting how some people attempt to rationalize violent or destructive behavior with this saying. This isn't a license to hex; it simply tells us that it is not the energy or power used that determines whether the result is healing or hexing. The energy is the same. The energy comes first. It is the intent that follows that makes the difference.

The fact is that the followers of some other religions regularly use magick against others in their community. These magickians presume that those community members have the capacity to use magick (or access to others that do) to negate the magick or defend themselves. Yet the average person in our Western society doesn't realize that they have this ability. Even if they did, such behavior would be contrary to the Wiccan Rede. Karma would ensure that there would be a price to pay for such behavior.

As a police officer, I often run into people who have suffered a number of misfortunes and setbacks in their lives. It is amazing how often these people will lay the blame for their misfortunes on crossed stars, bad luck, or "psychic attack." They expend vast quantities of energy on trying to improve their luck. They put up psychic wards and fire off energetic salvoes at those they hold responsible for their troubles. If things go wrong, they find someone or something else to blame. They resort to hexes and other forms of retribution. Journalist P. J. O'Rourke once aptly described this situation as follows:

> One of the annoying things about believing in free will and individual responsibility is the difficulty of finding somebody to blame your problems on. And when you do find somebody, it's remarkable how often his picture turns up on your driver's license.[6]

Many people never take the time to objectively examine their situation and take charge of their life. As I said earlier, a Warrior does not abandon herself to luck and fate. We all occasionally come up against obstacles and reversals. This is a part of living. There are some variables in life over which you have no control. The Warrior, however, places herself fully in charge of those things in her life that she does have control over. This offsets the effect of life's variables. We have control over many of the things that go wrong in our lives.

Wiccans are shapeshifters; we make adjustments to handle the situations that we find ourselves in. This is what shamans do. You shape your life and behavior to control life's circumstances to your advantage. We have to own up to our mistakes and our shortcomings and do something about them. Scott Cunningham put it very well when he rephrased the Rede to read, "Do nothing to harm yourself."[7] If you want to master your situation, you need to master yourself first. You are not at the mercy of the elements and fate unless you chose to be. You create your own reality.

This applies to helping other people too. You will definitely be in a better position to help others if you help yourself first. In this way, you will be operating from a solid foundation that will give you the strength you need to offer others support. "First things first" is the rule to follow here.

This leads us to the fifth Warrior Precept to note down in your Book of Shadows. This precept is to be found on Miyamoto Musashi's list:

Fifth Warrior Precept

Do not be negligent, even in trifling matters.

Attention to detail is one of the most effective ways to prevent unexpected problems. The Warrior plans for all possible contingencies. In a period of unexpected stress you will instinctively fall back on whatever plan you have prepared in advance. If you haven't planned or rehearsed for a problem you suddenly encounter, life will catch you like a deer in the headlights.

Another reason why this attention to Right Action and responsibility is important has to do with the Wiccan belief in reincarnation. Perfection is such a difficult objective to attain that we work toward it through many different lives. What we don't master in this life, we have to work on again in the next.

Don't blame problems in this life on past ones. Study your present life to identify recurring problems. These are the things that you are working on in this life. Go back over old journals, diaries, or letters to refresh your memory. Look for the mistakes that you seem to make over and over again. There is no need to do past-life regression to identify these problems. People have a tendency to romanticize past-life regression. They identify themselves with some notable person from the past rather than with a real person who has faults. I have encountered hordes of people who thought that in past lives they had been Cleopatra, Alexander the Great, Arthur, Nefertiti, Merlin, and other famous persons. Grandiose dreams of this sort won't do you much good. What happened in the past may be influencing you now, but what you do now is your responsibility. Later in this book we will examine more effective ways to deal with habits and obsessions.

Magickal Ethics

Before I do this, however, we should examine some of the ethics of magickal work.

First of all, try not to do magick for another without their permission. It is very difficult for anyone to know exactly what another person's situation and needs are. Remember that the Wiccan Rede makes you responsible for your actions. If what you do messes up another person's life, it is then your responsibility to set it right if you can.

A common example I've seen cited is the Wiccan who works healing magick for a terminally ill friend without first asking this friend if this is what he wants. If this friend were dying and longing for release from pain, using magick without his knowledge to keep him here may be contrary to his wishes. Such magick may cause him unnecessary suffering. Of course, there are also situations in which you may come across an unconscious person in need of immediate medical assistance. There is no way of knowing or determining what this person's wishes are in such a crisis situation. You must be the good Samaritan and do what you feel is best after considering the situation as carefully as time allows. The Wiccan Rede admonishes us to use our heads and be responsible.

One of the most common pitfalls in magick is the temptation to do magick to make someone fall in love with you. Only a fool magicks someone into loving them. It never works the way that you hope it will. The relationships created in this manner invariably lead to breakups that are hateful and ugly. This does not mean that you can't do magick to obtain a loving relationship. Just don't direct the magick at a particular person. The best results are based on the principle that "like attracts like." Put magick out there to attract the right partner to you. If the person that you think you have your eye on is that right person, well and good. If not, I assure you that you will attract a person who will be even better for you, as unlikely as that may seem at the time. I know. I magicked the universe and found my perfect partner in life. Remember this advice from Silver RavenWolf: "Never magick a person for something, magick the universe."[8]

In this chapter you've learned about chivalry and Right Action. You've learned about karma and the Law of Three-Fold Return. You've learned two new Warrior Precepts: (1) *Develop a sense of "Right Action;"* (2) *Do not be negligent, even in trifling matters.* We've discussed personal responsibility and magickal ethics. In the next chapter we will begin to look at some of the symbols of Wicca and how the Warrior uses them to achieve his ends.

Endnotes

1. Brian R. Price. (April 1997). "A Code of Chivalry: Modern, based on the 'Old Code,'" www.chronique.com/Library/Chivalry/code.htm.

2. Robin Wood. (1996). *When, Why . . . If*, p. 22.

3. Abigail Van Buren. (16 May 1974). "Dear Abby" syndicated newspaper column.

4. *Webster's New Twentieth Century Dictionary.*

5. Sir Arthur Conan Doyle. (1892). *Sherlock Holmes: The Complete Novels and Stories*, "The Speckled Band" (Bantam edition, 1986).

6. P. J. O'Rourke. (30 Nov. 1989). *Rolling Stone* magazine.

7. Scott Cunningham. (1989). *Wicca: A Guide for the Solitary Practitioner*, p. 5.

8. Silver RavenWolf. (2000). *Teen Witch: Wicca for a New Generation*, p. 135.

5

Symbols of Spirit

> *In a symbol there is concealment and yet revelation: here therefore, by silence and by speech acting together, comes a double significance. . . . In the symbol proper, what we can call a symbol, there is ever, more or less distinctly and directly, some embodiment and revelation of the Infinite; the Infinite is made to blend itself with the Finite, to stand visible, and as it were, attainable there.*
>
> Thomas Carlyle, *Sartor Resartus*, "Teufelsdröckh"

SYMBOLS ARE WHAT make ritual and mythology so powerful. This is because images and symbols are the language of the subconscious. British scientist J. B. S. Haldane told us that "words are well adapted for description and the arousing of emotion, but for many kinds of precise thought other symbols are much better."[1] Words are the language of the conscious mind, not the subconscious. A competent Wiccan uses symbols in ritual and magick to speak to the subconscious mind. This links the conscious and subconscious together to make your magick more effective.

To a certain extent, symbols are a very private concern. For example, if you are trying to interpret the symbolism of your dreams, you must first learn the unique symbolism of your mind. Dream symbols that mean something very definite to you may mean quite another thing to another person. We all have different experiences to draw from. The poet Baudelaire pointed out that "the whole visible universe is but a storehouse of images and signs to which the imagination will give a relative place and value; it is a sort of pasture which the imagination must digest and transform."[2] You have to figure out what images and signs are in the storehouse of your mind before you can make sense of them.

Keeping a journal of your dreams is a good way to start learning the symbols of your subconscious. Some people have difficulty doing this; they can't remember their dreams when they awaken. I find that it helps if before you go to sleep you make a conscious commitment to yourself to remember your dreams when you get up in the morning. It also helps if you keep a notepad or tape recorder handy at bedside. This way you can immediately set these dreams down when you awaken while they are still fresh in your mind. After awhile, you will be able to identify recurring themes and make connections to everyday events in your life.

Groups of people may identify particular symbols as significant to them. Over the years these symbols gather meaning and significance with use. Different groups may use the same symbol to mean quite different things. In other words, we learn what many symbols mean to us.

The swastika is a perfect example of this process. The swastika is an ancient symbol that has been in use since at least 10,000 B.C.E. It has appeared in religious art in India, Japan, Greece, Rome, Asia Minor, China, Persia, Libya, Scandinavia, Iceland, the British Isles, and in Native American cultures. The Greeks called the swastika the *Gammadion,* since it appeared to be composed of four Greek gammas, and they considered it a sacred symbol. In India it is known as the *Dorje.* Drawn with arms pointing clockwise the swastika was regarded as a solar symbol. Drawn with counterclockwise arms (a Sauvastika) it represented the moon or the feminine. Variations in medieval art include the Croix Gamme, Gamma Cross or Gammadion, the Fulfot or Fylfot, the Croix Cramponee, and the Germanic Hakenkreuz.

Adolf Hitler adopted the swastika as part of the symbolism of the Nazi party prior to the Second World War. Hitler did this on the assumption that the swastika was an "Aryan" symbol. Hitler was probably influenced by the eight-armed swastika that had long been the symbol of the ancient German Inquisitional society, the Vehmgericht. The Nazi use of the swastika has taught most people in modern Western society to associate it with evil. As you can see, this was not its original connotation at all.

The Pentagram, the symbol of Wicca, is a five-pointed star formed by five straight lines, with one point uppermost, enclosed within a circle. As the Pentagram consists of a continuous line that runs from point to point, it has been referred to as an "endless knot." It has taken thousands of years for the Pentagram to evolve into this modern symbol. The Pentagram is a very old symbol that has gradually gathered meaning unto itself over the centuries. I describe this development in the glossary at the end of the book (see page 239).

To the modern Wiccan, each of the five points of the Pentagram represents one of the five traditional elements: Spirit (represented by the top point), followed by (in order clockwise) Water, Fire, Earth, and Air. As Spirit is represented by the topmost point, the Pentagram is said to represent the dominion of Spirit over the other four elements and the supremacy of reason over matter. As the Pentagram represents both the five elements and, as pointed out, the human form, it reminds us of how we are all linked to the universe around us. As I pointed out earlier, unlike dualistic religions that hold that divinity is separate from the everyday world, Wicca is a religion of monism. Wiccans believe that the divine and the mundane are inseparably linked. Thus the

Pentagram symbolizes for us the means by which we may take control of our lives. We are already linked to the elements around us. We only need to recognize these links and make use of them.

Some symbols are universal. These are what Jung called "archetypes." They are symbols that occur in all cultures and in all times. Many of the aspects of deity that we use are archetypes of this sort. The concept of a Warrior is a universal archetype that I'm teaching you to access in this work.

The circle that encloses the Pentagram is a universal symbol. It symbolizes many things. As the circle has no beginning or end, it is a symbol of eternity. As it encloses the Pentagram within, it serves as another reminder that all of the five elements are linked to one another. It represents the consecrated Circle within which the Wiccan practices her Craft.

Every religion has a sacred place to practice their rituals in. For many religions this is a permanent structure: a temple, church, mosque, etc. What makes these places sacred is the belief of the people who use it. It is the belief of the adherent using them that makes them holy. In other words, these places are sacred because you make a conscious choice to make them so. This follows the Warrior Precept that I mentioned earlier: you create your own reality. The sacred space is itself a symbol that takes on the meaning that we give it.

Wiccans create their sacred space when and where they need it by casting a Circle. This underscores one of the two differences between sacred space as Wiccans use it and sacred space as it is usually used in the world's religions—the difference between the aforementioned permanent structures and the Wiccan Circle is that the latter is portable. It is sacred space that can be created anywhere at will. Wiccans are perhaps more conscious of this concept than the followers of some other religious faiths, since Wiccans have to recreate their sacred space every time they use it.

That the Wiccan is creating this sacred space in their mind brings out the other difference. We can also create a psychic or astral temple for ourselves that only exists in our mind. What happens in that astral temple affects what happens in the real world. As above, so below. I will tell you how to create such an astral temple as part of the visualization exercises in chapter 15. For now, let's look at the physical Circle.

Find a quiet and private space to set up your Circle. Outdoors is preferable, as it is easier to imagine your connection with nature in nature. You can cast a Circle in your backyard, in a secluded grove in a public park, or on a sandy beach. If this is not practical due to the weather or to nosy neighbors, find yourself a suitable place indoors. Some Wiccans reserve one room of their house for magickal work. They prefer to have a space that is consecrated and uncontaminated. Yet many of us do not have the luxury of having an extra room to use for such a purpose. Others clear out the living room or dining room for use. Even if the room is used for many purposes you may want to set up a permanent altar or niche in the room.

In ceremonial magick, the Circle is primarily used for protection. The ceremonial magickian is trying to keep the energy out. Their practices derive from a dualistic system that treats energy as an external force. The Wiccan Circle is primarily designed to contain magickal energy. For Wiccans, magick is an internal process.

Traditionally the Wiccan Circle is said to be nine feet in diameter. This is because the number nine is the number of the Moon in numerology. A Circle this size works very well for the solitary Wiccan, but is rather a cramped space for more than a handful of people. There is no size restriction; make your Circle as big as you need it to be. At festivals I have seen ritual Circles large enough to accommodate hundreds of people.

Each of the cardinal points of the Wiccan Circle corresponds to one of the five elements, to one side of the Witch's Pyramid, and to one of the Magickal Weapons (which I will discuss in chapter 7):

◆ East\Air\To Will\Athame

◆ South\Fire\To Imagine\Wand

◆ West\Water\To Dare\Chalice

◆ North\Earth\To Keep Silent\Pentacle

◆ Center\Spirit\To Know\Mind

Spirit is situated in the center of the Circle to symbolize the fact that spirit holds the other four elements together. The four cardinal points on the perimeter of the Circle are often marked with candles. If you so chose, these candles may be in colors appropriate to the elements involved.

In the center of the Circle is an altar. Traditionally in ceremonial magick this altar is three-foot square cube: half the height of a six-foot man. Like the cardinal points of the Circle, its four sides symbolize the elements of Air, Fire, Water, and Earth. Its top represents Spirit, and this is where the Wiccan displays other elemental symbols to reinforce this connection: a bowl of salt in the north for Earth, a censer of incense in the east for Air, a candle in the south for Fire, and a bowl of water in the west for Water. The Magickal Weapons, or working tools, are arranged in a similar fashion.

The altar is divided into two sides; the left side is that of the Goddess, and the right side is for the God. Many Wiccans display suitable statuary or pictures on these sides of the altar to represent the divine energy being used in the ritual. You may simply use a candle on each side of the altar to represent these deities.

We will discuss the actual casting of the Circle in chapter 10, since this is an energetic exercise. We need to discuss how to raise the energy involved before we attempt it. Before we do this, however, we can look at some of the occasions when a Wiccan commonly casts a Circle.

Esbats

The name that Wiccans give to the ritual observances held in Circle at the full moon is Esbats. It was the Egyptologist Margaret Murray who first used the term "Esbats" to describe mundane gatherings of Witches. She obtained it from the Old French term *Esbatment,* which means "to divert oneself" or "an amusement." Esbats are regular meetings where Wiccans cast Circles to celebrate, share energy, discuss business, perform tasks such as healing, and enjoy each others' company.

Through Esbats the Wiccan Warrior becomes attuned to the lunar cycles of this world. There are thirteen Esbats in the course of a year, one for each of the full moons. Much of the Wiccan's magick is performed during Esbats. This allows the Wiccan to tap into the energy of the waxing moon. It is a good monthly opportunity to review your progress, establish new goals, and work on current ones.

Doing magick at an Esbat is not a hard-and-fast rule. New Moon rituals are often referred to as "Dark Moon" ceremonies. Rituals may be performed during the first quarter (called "Diana's Bow") or the last quarter (called "Hecate's Sickle"), depending on what kind of work the Wiccans involved wish to accomplish. Different phases of the moon are appropriate for different purposes:

- ◆ *New Moon*—A good time to do magick for beginnings or for the initiation of new enterprises; the undertaking will grow as the moon waxes. This is also a good time for divination.

- ◆ *Waxing Moon*—An excellent time to do magick involving growth, healing, or increase.

- ◆ *Full Moon*—Represents a project coming to fruition, completion, or fulfillment.

◆   *Waning Moon*—Magick for cleansing, banishing, or completion.

For example, the period of the waning moon is considered by Wiccans to be a good time to work on banishing negative influences from your life.

Sabbats

Wiccans attune themselves to solar energy and celebrate the changing seasons of the year with eight High Holidays, or festivals, called Sabbats. These Sabbats are spaced evenly throughout the year.

Four of these High Holidays are Lesser Sabbats: These are the equinoxes and solstices. These are recent additions to the Wiccan calendar, originally being mostly Saxon holidays. Four of these High Holidays are the Greater Sabbats, which fall between these Lesser ones. These Greater Sabbats are the older, traditional Celtic holidays. The Greater Sabbats are fire festivals, at which bonfires are commonly lit (see glossary for the origin of the term bonfire, page 228). The Greater Sabbats fall on what we Wiccans call the "Cross-Quarter Days." The ancients noticed that at the cross-quarter days the length of days either noticeably started:

◆   Shortening or lengthening at a much faster rate (for example, after August 1 or February 2); or

◆   Shortening or lengthening at a much slower rate (for example, after October 31 or April 30).

If you graph the length of the days through the year, you end up with a sine curve and can see this for yourself. The Greater Sabbats were important days in the calendars of herding peoples such as the Celts. For example, Imbolc (February 2) marked the beginning of the lambing season. The Lesser Sabbats, on the other hand, were dates important to farming peoples. For example, Mabon, the autumnal equinox, is a harvest festival.

In accordance with ancient Celtic tradition, Wiccans normally consider the day as beginning at sundown and ending at the following sundown. Thus the Sabbat of Samhain runs from sundown on October 31 to sundown on November 1. This is why it later received the name "All Hallows Eve"—it starts in the evening and ends the next.

To the Warrior, the passing of the eight Sabbats marks more than just the turning of the seasons. Sabbats aren't just celebrations to the Warrior. The turning seasons of the wheel of the year reflect the pattern of resolution-commitment-action-review that the Warrior uses to maximize effectiveness. They are landmarks in the progress of the Warrior. The manner in which the seasons fit into this cycle are examined in the other four books in this work. I will describe these Sabbats and their connection to the Warrior later in this work. Two Sabbats, one Greater and one Lesser, are paired in each of the books that follows. I won't go into the ritual observances Wiccans perform on the Sabbats in this work; ritual is a vast subject that deserves a separate book.

Now we have examined the symbols: personal, learned, and universal. You've learned how to study the symbols in your dreams. We've discussed the symbolism of the Pentagram and the Circle. We've examined sacred space and the Esbats and Sabbats. We have learned how the Wiccan is linked to the lunar and solar cycles of nature. In the next chapter we will learn how to raise magickal energy and use it to cast the Circle.

Endnotes

1. J. B. S. Haldane. (1932). *The Inequality of Man*, "God-Makers."
2. Charles Baudelaire. (1868; repr. in *The Mirror of Art*, ed. by Jonathan Mayne, 1955). "Salon of 1859," sct. 3, in *Curiosités Esthétiques.*

6

Experiencing Energy

The human body is an energy system . . . which is never a complete structure; never static; is in perpetual inner self-construction and self-destruction; we destroy in order to make it new.

Norman O. Brown, "Love's Body"

IN THIS CHAPTER I want to begin speaking about the subject of sending out energy. This concept is related to two sides of the Witch's Pyramid: *To Dare* and *To Will.* The other half is grail magick—the capacity to be filled by the divine energy. This "drawing in" relates to two of the sides of the Witch's Pyramid: *To Keep Silent* and *To Imagine* (more on this later).

A Warrior needs to become sensitive to the energy within and without. You must connect to the channels of energy around you and let it flow through you in order to do magick effectively. This reduces the stress on your physical reserves. The trick is to tap into the natural energy around you and use this instead of your personal reserves. Here is another way of looking at this process. You are constantly immersed in a sea of life energy. It is omnipresent.

What you have to do is become a valve or a gateway to let this energy funnel through you as you direct it with your will. The energy that you use in magick flows through you.

In Asian medicine and martial arts energy is called "chi" or "ki." I encourage you to practice techniques from disciplines such as Chi Kung that get this energy, or chi, circulating in your body. This will allow you to feel what it is like to have the chi flowing through you. This in turn will makes it easier for you to use other energy-raising techniques in or out of Circle. You'll know when the energy is flowing because you have experienced it in another application. You don't have to wait to see if your magick has been effective. Awareness of the energy flow during the magickal working gives you a much better indication of how effective your magick is at the time that you are practicing it.

To work magick, you must focus energy at your objective with your will. If you have no energy to focus, you aren't going to get very far. As I have already pointed out, in my workshops and classes I teach some basic techniques derived from the martial arts to let the participants experience the chi coursing through their bodies. It is amazing how many of these people report to me afterward that they have never felt anything like this before. Some of these people have been practicing Wicca for years. Previously, when doing their magick, they had not felt anything like this rush of energy. So before I go into details about what to do with energy in magick, let me show you some ways to raise the energy to use.

There is an old Zen adage, *Ken-Zen Ichi Nyo* ("Body and Mind Together"). You cannot separate the mental and magickal processes from the physical one. Magickal energy will best flow through you if your body is in good shape. Everything in your environment—mental, physical, emotional, and spiritual—affects both how you raise energy and how this energy affects you. This leads us to the sixth Warrior Precept:

Sixth Warrior Precept

Your body is your temple. Care for it!

A healthy body is better able to channel energy than an unhealthy one. You don't need to be a rocket scientist to see that a person who is in good shape has better reserves of energy than someone who is unfit and infirm. If your body is healthy, the functioning of your mind is more likely to be healthy too. The better shape that you are in, the more effective your magick will be. Chi flows more efficiently through a body that is fit. Your body is a reflection of the divinity with which you are connected. What better way to acknowledge this divinity than to respect this gift of life that you have been given? The expression "Thou art God" takes on a whole new meaning if you look in the mirror and don't like what you see looking back.

Many of the Eastern forms of medicine and religion include systems for manipulating and improving the flow of life energy or chi through the body. I highly recommend using systems of exercise such as Chi Kung to improve both your health and the flow of energy through you.

I also recommend that you take the time to do a daily devotion. A daily devotion will help you focus your attention on the body that carries the divine spark that is you. You can use this devotion when you get up in the morning, or before you go to work. You can devise your own devotion using any words suitable to your situation. Here is an example to use:

> Blessed be my feet that are set upon Her path.
>
> Blessed be my knees, which hold me proud and strong.
>
> Blessed be my heart, which gives me courage.
>
> Blessed by my hands, which fashion what I imagine.

Blessed be my lips, that they may speak the truth.

Blessed be my eyes, that they may perceive reality.

Blessed be my ears, that they may hear new lessons.

May I find the Lady and the Lord within me.

Let me do things to bring honor upon them and me
this day.

Devotions such as this can help you to focus on the care of your body. This will have a profound effect on your ability to raise and direct energy to do magick.

What you eat has profound effects on your ability to raise energy, too. For example, fasting has traditionally been used by many religious groups as a means to bring on visions and trance states. People forced by necessity into survival situations where food is scarce or nonexistent will have experienced the effects of this too. I have had vivid experiences of this sort both in my Air Force survival training and in subsequent observations made when teaching survival techniques to air and army cadets. Variations in blood-sugar levels have profound effects on people. People with children are certainly familiar with the sugar rush that can send their kids chasing around the room. Diabetics having an insulin reaction are another common example. Within minutes they can go from a raving belligerent to a mild-mannered person as the paramedics administer aid. One of the reasons that the Wiccan ceremony of "cakes and wine" is included at the end of the ritual is that the consumption of food tends to ground us (more on this later).

Therefore an exercise program should be supported with a healthy diet. A high-fat diet consisting of processed food, or an excess of caffeine, tobacco, or alcohol will affect your energetic levels and thought processes. A balanced, healthy diet will help to stabilize your energy and clarify your mind. This, in turn, will make your magick more effective.

Energy Exercises

Your posture also affects the flow of energy through your body. This statement will not be news to anyone who has studied yoga or Asian medicine. Let's look at a very simple posture that will remove any blockages and maximize your energetic output in magick, which is often called "Entering Tranquility."

Stand with your feet about shoulder-width apart, toes pointing forward. Shift your weight slightly forward on to the balls of your feet. Do not lock your knees. By this I do not mean having them so loose that you collapse in a heap; just don't make them rigid. Keep your knees spread apart slightly, as if you were sitting on a horse. Don't allow your knees to flex inward. It helps to imagine that you have something like a basketball held between your knees, keeping them apart. Keep your abdomen relaxed and "soft."

Breathe naturally into your lower lungs, letting your abdomen naturally expand and contract. Don't breathe by flexing your chest; use your diaphragm instead. Have you ever noticed how an infant breathes when she is on her back? Her stomach rises and falls as she breathes. In Western society we learn to breathe with our chests as we mature. I don't want you to breathe with your chest here. I want you to breathe down into your abdomen.

Now imagine that someone has attached a string to the top of your head and is pulling upward. This will straighten your back and roll your backside under your spine to support it better. Let your arms hang at your sides with the palms turned to face behind you. Lightly touch the tip of your tongue to the roof of your mouth.

In this posture all of the energy channels are free. It is common to experience tingling or sensations of heat or cold in your arms when the chi is flowing. When you are doing magick, you should feel this energy flow. If you don't, check to see what is blocking the energy flow and correct it.

Notice that I am asking you to relax in this posture. No part of your body is tense. Magick is not a matter of gritting your teeth, tensing your muscles, and forcing energy out of yourself. It is a matter of relaxing and letting the energy flow through you. Tensing yourself inhibits this flow.

If you get dizzy while trying to find the right rhythm for your breathing, you are hyperventilating. Slow your breathing rate down and this dizziness will disappear. Yawning isn't necessarily an indication that you are relaxing. It may be an indication that you are holding your breath too long on the inhalation part of the cycle. Coughing can be an indication that you are holding too long on the exhalation part of the cycle.

The Entering Tranquility posture can be used to center yourself before doing magickal or ritual work. As you exhale, imagine "dark air" or negative energy leaving your body. As you inhale, imagine "light air," "pure air," or positive energy entering your body. Continue until you are filled with pure energy and the dark energy is no longer flowing out of you.

Starting from this Entering Tranquility posture we can move into a number of different techniques to store up a charge of magickal energy. The first step is to imagine energy collecting between your palms with an exercise that I call "Forming a Ball." Do this exercise in the Entering Tranquility posture or sitting upright in a chair. Hold your palms a few inches apart in front of you and imagine a swirling ball of energy forming between them. Feel its pulse and its heat. Note its color. Let it gradually grow, pushing against your palms. Once your are done with it, press it into your abdomen in the region of your navel and re-absorb it. Record your impressions in your Book of Shadows.

The reason that I have you press your ball of energy into your abdomen to re-absorb it is that, in Asian medicine and martial arts, this area just behind and about three inches below the navel is an energy storage area known as the *Dantian*. There are four energy fields in the body in Chinese Chi Kung: *Yuanguan, Dantian, Niyuan,* and *Zhongyuan.* To the martial artist and the magickian, the Dantian is the most important. This energy storage area is the foundation of Tai Chi and Chi Kung practice.

Here is a useful variation of Forming the Ball for those in a group setting—let's call it "Passing the Ball." Have the members of the group sit in a circle. One person starts by Forming the Ball of energy in their hands. This person then passes the ball into the hands of the person beside him. The person receiving it notes the sensations and impressions that she feels. Pass the energy ball around the circle until it gets back to the person who made it. This person then re-absorbs or grounds the energy ball. Each person takes a turn Forming the Ball and passing it around. This not only gives you practice raising energy; it also allows you to practice sensing chi in other people. As you develop your practice you will come to learn that this is a useful skill. Record your impressions in your Book of Shadows.

You will note that in this technique I have you sending energy out of both of your hands and collecting it between them. Some people have observed that one hand is naturally a "projective" hand; that is, you tend to send your energy out of this one hand. The other hand is said to be receptive; that is, you tend to sense or draw in energy currents more easily with this hand. It is said that for right-handed people the right, or dominant, hand is the projective hand, while the left hand is the receptor. In left-handed people this is reversed. For the untrained person this probably holds true. However, just as in martial arts you learn to strike with either hand or foot, you can train yourself to project or receive with either hand. You should practice the use of both hands in both receiving and sending energy.

Now let's expand our earlier "Forming the Ball" exercise by developing it into a more advanced technique called "Holding the Ball." Starting from the Entering Tranquility posture, raise your arms in front of you as if encircling a large beach ball, holding it against your chest. Spread your fingers and don't let your hands touch. Imagine that you are clasping a ball of energy to your breast—a larger version of the small ball of energy you manipulated in the "Forming the Ball" exercise. As you inhale, it expands and glows; imagine the ball of energy pressing out against your arms and chest. As you exhale, it contracts and spins forward. Let this ball of energy grow for awhile. As before, when you are done, press the ball of energy that you have created into your abdomen to re-absorb it. Record your impressions of this exercise in your Book of Shadows.

Chakras

Chakra is a Hindu term meaning "wheels." In Hindu and Tantric metaphysics, chakras are the energy centers located along the spine. They are also known as *Padmas* ("lotuses"). From the lowest to the highest they are:

- *Muladhara*—A Sanskrit term meaning "the root base." This is the root chakra, located at the pelvic plexus between the anus and urethra. This is where the kundalini energy, or chi, is said to originate.

- *Swadhisthana*—A Sanskrit term meaning "one's own place," or "her favorite resort." Located at the hypogastric plexus behind the navel. This is the area known as the Dantian in Chi Kung. In Chinese medicine it is believed to be an energy-storage area.

- *Manipura*—A Sanskrit term meaning "gem city." Manipura is located at the solar plexus.

- *Anahata*—A Sanskrit term meaning "a sound that is not made by striking two things together." It is located at the cardiopulmonary plexus in the spine at the level of the nipples.

- *Vissudda*—A Sanskrit term meaning "purification" or "purity center." Located at a point in the spine opposite the larynx.

- *Ajna*—A Sanskrit term meaning "authority" or "command." Located at the pineal gland in the head, roughly between the ears and straight back behind a point between the eyebrows referred to as the "third eye."

- *Sahasrara*—A Sanskrit term meaning "thousand-petalled." Located at the top of the head.

- *Bindu* (also known as *Brahmarandra*)—A Sanskrit term meaning "semen." The highest of the chakras, located at the point just to the rear of the crown of the head. This is known in Chi Kung as the *baihui* ("meeting of a hundred meridians"). It is considered to be an energy safety valve in Chi Kung.

Energy starts at the root chakra, Muladhara, and rises up through the spinal cord, which is known as *Sushumna*. The energy passes through each of the other chakras, energizing each in turn. In Hindu mythology this energy is known as kundalini, and is symbolized by a coiled green snake. When the energy arrives at the top most chakra, Bindu, it then flows back down channels to either side of the spine called *ida* and *pingala*.

You can activate each of these energy centers separately. To start, place yourself in a relaxed posture such as Entering Tranquility. A prone position on your back is another option. Visualize breathing energy into each of your chakras, one at a time. Since the energy starts at Muladhara and rises up the spinal cord, it is best to start at Muladhara and work upward.

- *Muladhara*—Visualize this as a ball of *red* light. Once you sense that this chakra is activated, move on to . . .

- *Swadhisthana*—Visualize this as a ball of *orange* light. Once you sense that this chakra is activated, move on to . . .

◆ *Manipura*—Visualize this as a ball of *yellow* light. Once you sense that this chakra is activated, move on to . . .

◆ *Anahata*—Visualize this as a ball of *green* light. Once you sense that this chakra is activated, move on to . . .

◆ *Vissudda*—Visualize this as a ball of *blue* light. Once you sense that this chakra is activated, move on to . . .

◆ *Ajna*—Visualize this as a ball of *violet* light. Once you sense that this chakra is activated, move on to . . .

◆ *Sahasrara*—Visualize this as a ball of *indigo* light. Once you sense that this chakra is activated, finally move on to . . .

◆ *Bindu*—Visualize this as a ball of *white* light.

If you detect a blockage at any one of these chakras you can take a moment to activate it by visualizing the appropriately colored energy at that chakra. Blockages occurring at any of the chakras can affect this flow of energy as well as a person's physical health. Each of the chakras is connected to certain systems in the body:

◆ *Muladhara*—Pelvic plexus. Ovaries and testes.

◆ *Swadhisthana*—Hypogastric plexus. Suprarenal glands.

◆ *Manipura*—Solar plexus. Pancreas.

◆ *Anahata*—Cardiopulmonary plexus.

◆ *Vissudda*—Pharyngeal plexus. Thyroid and parathyroids.

◆ *Ajna*—Pineal gland.

◆ *Bindu*—Brain.

Later, in chapter 8, you will learn to sense these energy centers through your hands.

There are subchakras, or energy centers, in the body as well. For example, there are subchakras located in the palms and fingertips. We can send and receive sensory and energetic information through these subchakras. This is one of the reasons why I have been teaching you exercises requiring you to send and form energy with your hands. The energy naturally flows out of these subchakras. To translate this into Wiccan terms, let us examine the entire hand:

◆ *Thumb*—Corresponds to the element of Earth.

◆ *Middle finger*—Corresponds to the element of Fire. Later you will discover that the Wand and the Spear or Staff are Magickal Weapons of Fire. You can project energy from this finger in the same way that you can project it from a Wand or Staff.

◆ *Ring finger*—This finger corresponds to the element of Water.

◆ *Little finger*—This finger corresponds to the element of Spirit.

This is the basis for the magickal gestures that appear in many Asian systems, in which the fingers are interwoven in various patterns to make certain energetic "circuits." The exercises up until now have involved sending energy out of your palm with the fingers spread. If you consider the entire hand as representing your will, now you can see how you can fine-tune the energy being projected by pointing specific fingers and folding others against the palm. For example, I might send healing (Earth) energy into a colleague through my thumb.

Sharing Energy

How much energy is needed for a particular magickal project will depend on the size of the project. The larger the objective, the longer it will usually take for the magick to take effect. Larger goals may require months of magickal buildup in order for desires to manifest. This is one of the reasons that Wiccans operate in Covens; it gives them access to the energy of the group. The increased energy can speed up the magickal process.

Much is made of polarity of energy in some Wiccan traditions. Some will go to great lengths to pair up males and females as if this will somehow balance the energy involved. When the priestess is working, the priest sends her energy and vice versa. In over thirty years I've actually only rarely seen a Coven with a perfect balance of males and females. Even when I did, it usually didn't last; sooner or later people leave or new people join, throwing the balance out again. It doesn't have to be a male sending energy to a female or a female to a male. Anyone can send energy to anyone else regardless of sex. This is one of the duties of the Guardian in same gender Circles; the Guardians send energy to the Priest(ess).

Practice sending energy to one another within your group using the energy projecting exercises that I have shown you so far. Record the results in your Book of Shadows. Later, in the Book of Air, I will teach you other group techniques that you can use to share energy.

In this chapter you have learned various techniques for raising the energy that you will use in magick. You've learned to feel the energy within. We've discussed the importance of linking to the energy of the universe. You've learned a new Warrior Precept: *Your body is your temple.* Later we will come back to some of these techniques and show you their practical applications. But first we need to look at Magickal Tools and Weapons and how they are used in magick.

7

Magickal Tools and Magickal Weapons

> *But lo! Men have become the tools of their tools.*
>
> Henry David Thoreau, *Walden*

IN THIS WORK, as well as in my previous book, *Wiccan Warrior,* I have emphasized that the Warrior's path is a nonviolent one. Yet one cannot think of Warriors without thinking of weapons. When one studies the Asian martial arts, one may also study the bo, the sword, the tonfa, the nunchaku, and many other Warrior's tools.

Magickal Weapons are an element that Gerald Gardner borrowed from *Ceremonial Magick* when he laid down the basic structure of Wiccan ritual practice. In *Ceremonial Magick* they are often referred to as "Elemental Weapons."[1] The attitude of the Ceremonial Magickian is summed up in *The Greater Key of Solomon,* "In order to properly carry out the greatest and most important Operations of the Art, various Instruments are necessary . . ."[2] *The Greater Key of Solomon* instructs the magickian to "beat or strike the air" with his sword while making his conjurations and prayers.[3] Clearly the "instruments" of the art were considered weapons for the magickian's protection against the powers that he used.

Anyone who has experienced the Gardnerian first-degree initiation or at least read accounts of it will be familiar with the part of the ritual in which the Initiator presents the "Working Tools" to the Initiate:

> First, the Magic Sword. With this, as with the Athame, thou canst form all Magic Circles, dominate, subdue and punish rebellious spirits and demons, even persuade angels and good spirits. With this in thy hand, thou art the ruler of the Circle. Next I present the Athame. This is the true witch's weapon, and has all the powers of the Magic Sword.[4]

In this passage it is very clear that Gardner considers these working tools as Magickal Weapons. The Athame mentioned in this passage is a dagger used in Wiccan ritual (see the glossary, page 224). Such Weapons are part of a Judeo-Christian magickal system that treats energy as an external process. They believe that the magick Circle is primarily a means of defense against dangerous forces of nature. To the Wiccan Warrior, the forces (or energy) of nature are something that we let flow through us. It is an internal process. This being the case, why do we need Magickal Weapons? What are we protecting ourselves from?

I will suggest to you that what we need to protect ourselves from is our own nature. Weapons are not the cause of violence. It is how weapons are used that is crucial. For example, police officers like myself carry a selection of "force options" (to use the current jargon) to keep the peace. When faced with an aggressive offender, we police officers must chose the appropriate force option to effectively manage the level of force that the offender is using. We are criminally liable for excessive use of force. Many of these "force options," if used improperly, can cause serious injury, or even death. The Warrior must master the use of his weapons or they will master him.

Weapons aren't limited to what people ordinarily think of as weapons. As anyone who has studied Karate can tell you, the empty hand is an effective weapon (that's what the name Karate means, "empty hand"). The most common weapon used in domestic violence is not a gun or knife. It is whatever is within reach of the assailant. Weapons don't commit violent acts. People do. This underscores the responsibility involved in the Warrior's path. The Warrior's path is a peaceful one because he wills it to be so.

I am not advocating the use of weapons here. At work I must carry a firearm, but I'm solidly behind gun control. The point that I'm trying to make is that weapons become an extension of ourselves. In their use we learn something of the user. So I refer to the tools found in the typical Pagan ritual as Magickal Weapons. I do this to emphasize the fact that if misused, these tools can cause a lot of pain and suffering. By naming them Weapons we remind ourselves that they should be respected and used properly, lest we do unintended harm.

For the Wiccan Warrior, there are several sets of Magickal Weapons that have been adopted from Celtic mythology. Steve Blamires grouped these Weapons into four double groups in his book *Glamoury*.[5] I have modified his groupings in my practice: I have identified five double groupings. This is because Blamires did not include Spirit as one of the elements in his list.

In my system, each group of Magickal Weapons is associated with an element. For Air (east), the dagger (Athame) or Sword. For Fire (south), the Wand or Spear. For Water (west), the Chalice or Cauldron. For Earth (north), the Pentacle (see the glossary, page 238), Shield or Stone. The Magickal Weapon of Spirit is the Warrior's mind. Note that I will spell the word "Weapon" beginning with a capital *W* in this work when I am using the word in reference to a Magickal Weapon.

These Magickal Weapons can be grouped into two categories, Greater and Lesser, as follows.

Greater Magickal Weapons

◆ Spirit

◆ Sword

◆ Spear

◆ Cauldron

◆ Shield

Lesser Magickal Weapons

◆ Mind

◆ Athame (dagger)

◆ Wand

◆ Chalice

◆ Pentacle or Stone

In this chapter we will focus on the most important of the five Magickal Weapons: Spirit and Mind. We will examine the other four Magickal Weapons later in this work.

Spirit is the source of the energy that the Warrior accesses in magickal work. It is Spirit that gives the Warrior access to the other four elements. This is why I have classified Spirit as a Greater Magickal Weapon. A wooden pole can be a broom handle or a quarterstaff depending on how it is used. Similarly, the energy is just energy; it is the intent that determines whether it becomes healing or destructive.

The mind is the key. It is your mind that provides this intent. It is your mind that allows you to access and use the Magickal Weapons and all of the elements. I am reminded of the scene in the movie *Braveheart* in which uncle Argyle is speaking to the young William Wallace. "First I'll teach you how to use this," he says, tapping William on the head with his finger, "Then I'll teach you how to use this," he continues, showing William his broadsword. The lesson in this is that the mind is the key to the mastery of Magickal Weapons. The interesting thing is that the mind can ultimately replace all of them.

I know a lot of Wiccans who surround themselves with ritual tools and paraphernalia such as these Magickal Weapons. Their Covensteads and Circles are crammed full of all manner of props and ritual gear, as if they were practicing Occidental Ceremonial Magick. In Ceremonial Magick, precise rituals and specific props, paraphernalia, and symbols are usually believed to be necessary to successfully practice magick.

I briefly described this process in my book *Wiccan Warrior.* Many people become so dependent on this ritual gear that they cannot practice magick without it. Dependence on tools is a very human characteristic. "Man is a tool-using animal," said Thomas Carlyle, "Without tools he is nothing, with tools he is all."[6] I find that this human characteristic can often lead to overdependence on tools in magick, however.

This leads us to the seventh Warrior Precept to note down in your Book of Shadows:

Seventh Warrior Precept
Minimal appearance, maximum content.

In Hollywood action movies, the fight scenes are full of exaggerated, flashy moves. Stunt people go bouncing off of springboards doing soaring kicks. Serious martial artists and police officers will tell you that, in real life, the best moves are the most subtle ones. The best moves are quick, hard to see, and devastatingly effective. I apply this principle to my practice of magick. You don't need to do complicated, lengthy rituals to do effective magick. The best approach is to adhere to the K.I.S.S. principle (Keep It Simple and Straightforward).

In the prologue I pointed out the similarity between a defini-tion of magick ("Causing change by directing energy with one's will") and the old Karate adage ("Chi follows I"). The perfect strik-ing technique is 80–90 percent chi. This chi is directed to the tar-get by the will or intent (I) of the martial artist. Your punch is therefore not a bony hammer, but a connecting bridge channeling the chi from you to the opponent. Ideally, only a small portion of the technique is physical strength. That is where I came up with the concept of full contact magick. Obviously in combat this energy is accessed instantaneously. It wouldn't be of any use to the martial artist if you could not.

In one series of workshops that I conducted, I would ask the participants how many of them practiced their magick in Circle. Invariably all of the hands in the room would go up. I would then get the participants to confirm the general pattern of this proce-dure; they would go through an elaborate process of cleansing, setting up the altar, circumambulating with the elements, calling the quarters, drawing down the deities, performing some energy-raising technique, and sending out the energy. The whole process is then reversed as the magickian closes down the Circle.

Now, when the martial artist in the middle of a fight decides to launch a punch or kick, she doesn't first go through an elaborate process of cleansing, setting up altars, circumambulating with the elements, calling the quarters, drawing down the deities, etc. She instantaneously connects with the energy and sends it out through her fist or foot. The whole process of energizing and focusing with the will takes a split second.

You are probably now asking yourself, "What point is he trying to make here?" Ask yourself this: How much of the ritual exercise that you went through to cast that elaborate Circle with all of those magickal props had anything to do with the raising and directing of energy? The answer is not much.

I see so many people get lost in elaborate rituals as if it was simply this process alone that was creating the energy used in the magick. You can do magick where you are right now without any Circle, without any paraphernalia, without any ritual. All you have to do is raise energy and direct it. Marco Rodriquez, a fellow police officer and Ceremonial Magickian, once put it this way, "If it was the tools that made magick, we'd be mechanics, not magickians."[7]

I'm not suggesting that you should abandon ritual and sell off all of your ritual gear. Quite the contrary. Ritual is a very effective tool and I encourage my students to master it. Many of the ritual implements used in the typical Wiccan Circle can be used to focus and enhance the working, too. In the four Books that follow, I'll show you techniques for using these Magickal Weapons. Yet we need to be very clear about one thing: The bottom line is that you only need one thing to raise and direct energy—yourself. You are the source of the energy.

So why use ritual tools at all? The answer is that ritual tools like Magickal Weapons can be used to help focus magickal energy. Like the weapons that you practice with in the dojo, they can be used as extensions of yourself. They don't raise and direct the energy; you do. Once you have developed the ability to raise energy and let it flow from you, Magickal Weapons can be used to help you direct it.

Let's look at an example of such a focussing tool. One of the most common techniques of Wiccan magick involves candles. Candles of particular colors are selected, decorated, anointed, and lit. It isn't the candle that is generating the magick. You are. It isn't the candle that is directing the magickal energy to its source. Again, you are. Yet during the course of the ritual and later in the course of your day, your mind keeps coming back to the recollection that this candle is steadily burning on the altar. This repetitive recollection intensifies your magick as it brings your intent back into focus again and again. You are doing the magick. The candle is just a tool that you are using to help you do it.

Another thing that this ritual paraphernalia does for us is to help us create the sacred space that we use—the Circle. Wiccans either dress up in ritual robes or get skyclad (naked) to do ritual. These actions are a signal to the subconscious that something special is happening, as these actions are something out of the ordinary routine of our lives. By surrounding ourselves with ritual paraphernalia, we are encircling ourselves with things that remind us what our purpose is in that ritual Circle. This helps those of us with less experience focus on the task at hand.

Another purpose behind magickal paraphernalia is to help us feel magickal. In order to appear magickal you must think that you are magickal. Putting on that magickal robe or doing ritual skyclad is a signal to your mind as well as the world that you are accessing the Magickian archetype. Besides, many people find that it is fun to dress up. Religious observances should be a joyous experience. As my wife Phoenix McFarland says, "If you aren't having fun in your religion you are either doing the wrong religion or you are doing your religion wrong."

All of the tools that you commonly find in a magick Circle, like crystals or Magickal Weapons, have varying levels of energy stored in them. You have a certain amount of personal energy stored up in your body, too, at any given moment. Yet, if you rely on these tools or on your body alone, you will quickly deplete these sources. You will quickly wear yourself out. It is possible to draw the energy or chi out of yourself without connecting to the universe around you. However, if you do this, your reserves of energy will be limited to those stored within you. This is a common mistake with beginners. They quickly run their "batteries" dry.

I recently did a lengthy series of shifts reading Tarot at the Llewellyn booth at Book Expo America. Several staff members commented on my stamina. They couldn't understand why I hadn't worn myself out. The reason was that I was tapping into the chi around me rather than relying on my own reserves. This is why I am putting such emphasis on learning to start the energy flowing through you in this book.

The mind is the Warrior's ultimate tool. Mind is the Lesser Magickal Weapon of Spirit. It is the mind that accesses all of the five sides of the Witch's Pyramid. It is the mind that knows. It is the mind that dares. It is the mind that imagines. Will is the power of the mind. Of all the Greater Magickal Weapons, the mind is the most important.

People like me tend toward the "Hermetic" end of the magickal spectrum; we practice magick through mental, psychic, and spiritual development and dispense with magickal paraphernalia as much as possible. Others surround themselves with magickal accessories. You will find whatever system is most effective for you in time.

Call them Magickal Weapons or call them Magickal Tools, either way they are training wheels. Ultimately we strive to achieve the mastery that will allow us to lay these tools aside and do without them.

You've learned what Magickal Weapons are and the importance of respecting them. I've emphasized the peaceful nature of the Warrior's path. You've learned about the Greater and Lesser Magickal Weapons. You've learned that Spirit and Mind are the most important Magickal Weapons. I've discussed how much to rely on magickal tools. You've learned the Warrior Precept: *Minimal appearance, maximum content.* Finally you've learned that Magickal Weapons are used to focus energy, not create it. Now that we have examined the world of Spirit, it is time to move on to the world of Earth.

Endnotes

1. Dion Fortune. (1978). *Moon Magic,* p. 80.

2. *The Greater Key of Solomon,* bk. 2, ch. 8, introductory paragraph.

3. *The Greater Key of Solomon,* bk. 1, ch. 3.

4. Janet Farrar and Stewart Farrar. (1984). *A Witches Bible,* Volume II: The Rituals, p. 19.

5. Steve Blamires. (1995). *Glamoury: Magic of the Celtic Green World,* p. 292.

6. Thomas Carlyle. (1833–34). *Sartor Resartus,* bk. 1, ch. 5.

7. E-mail to me from Officer Marco Roderiguez of the LAPD, 3-31-00.

Book Two

THE BOOK OF EARTH

ARTH IS THE essential clay from which we were formed and to which we must ultimately return. Earth is our foundation, our beginning, and our end. The element of Earth is related to the business of living. To survive we must have the food, shelter, and clothing that Mother Earth provides. It is a feminine element; life is born out of the womb of Mother Earth. The symbol of Earth is the Pentacle; its coin shape symbolizes worth, reward, and the treasures of Earth. This includes our perception of our worth as human beings. Thus, the Wiccan Warrior's first task outside of the realm of Spirit is to get his "Earth altar" in order. You must re-establish your connection with the natural world. For it is the element of Earth that gives the Wiccan Warrior power in the physical plane. In the Wiccan's Circle, the element of Earth is found in the north. Gnomes are the spirits of Earth. The color of the element of Earth is green, symbolizing the life that springs from it.

What our eyes behold may well be the text of life but one's meditations on the text and the disclosures of these meditations are no less a part of the structure of reality.

Wallace Stevens, "The Necessary Angel"

8

To Keep Silent

No two people see the external world in exactly the same way. To every separate person a thing is what he thinks it is; in other words, not a thing, but a think.

Penelope Fitzgerald, "The Fate of Angels"

WE NOW SHIFT from the realm of Spirit into the material world. Everything here is made of energy, too. It is our perception that makes things seem solid. In the Book of Spirit we learned how to raise and feel energy. Before we use this energy, we must learn the lessons of Earth. It is here we learn the meaning of one side of the Witch's Pyramid: *To Keep Silent*.

The lesson implied by this side of the Witch's Pyramid can be summed up in the eighth Warrior Precept to write down in your Book of Shadows.

Eighth Warrior Precept

Perceive that which cannot be seen with the eye.

The first of the five principles that form the Witch's Pyramid that we discussed was *To Know*. Knowing comes from awareness. I told you earlier that the Goddess and the God will speak to you if you will just take the time to listen. One cultivates this awareness in silence.

It is said that "silence is the warrior's art and meditation is his sword."[1] To keep silent is to become still within and without. To clear your mind of distractions. To become aware of subtle currents, instincts, and emotions. To see into the depths not only of the world around you, but into the depths of human nature, too. Earlier we spoke of knowing being awareness. To keep silent is to become pure awareness.

This is one of the two sides of the Witch's Pyramid (the other being *To Imagine*) that is concerned with the grail process of drawing in energy. You become silent in order to sense the energy currents around you so that you can allow the energy to fill you. Remember what I told you in the chapter about experiencing energy? You want this energy to flow through you so that you can direct it out again with your will.

Psychologists use the word "flow" to describe the fluidity people experience in meditation. Flow states are moments when we are at our best. Living is awareness. Our perception is normally about 70 percent vision with the remaining 30 percent divided between the four senses of hearing, smell, touch, and taste. Warriors use meditation to enhance their perceptions and bring all four senses up to maximum perceptive levels.

The purpose of meditation is to train and discipline your mind so that you can use this Lesser Magickal Weapon more effectively and efficiently. You must train your mind to be still. There is an old saying in Karate, "Mind like water, mind like the moon." The mind must be like a still pond, conscious of the slightest ripple, able to accurately reflect reality. Bruce Lee encouraged the Warrior to "observe what is with undivided awareness."[2] Satori is the Warrior's state of being. A mind free of thought. Pure awareness.

The Warrior must learn to wait patiently. This was a very important principle to the ancient Samurai. The weaker swordsman, unable to stand the strain of waiting, often tried to deal the first blow. In an instant he revealed his strategy to his opponent. It was only then that his more patient and skilled opponent would strike, using a blow that was a combination of parry and attack, calculated to neutralize the strategy revealed by the less-patient opponent. To stand face-to-face with an enemy armed with four feet of razor-sharp steel in this fashion required endless patience and awesome concentration. This endurance and diligence will intensify your magick.

This is a lesson I learned early in police work. To stand silent and aware while the suspect is taunting, insulting, and otherwise trying to distract you gives you a distinct advantage. You can read the person's body language and sense his energy if you don't focus on the abusive and derogatory behavior. It doesn't distract you from what the suspect is actually doing. This allows you to respond quicker and use less force to control him should he become violent. Often it permits you to deal with the situation without resorting to physical means at all.

Such enhanced states of awareness are certainly altered states compared to normal waking consciousness—a form of trance state. Obviously trance states can also be achieved by using drugs; drugs alter your consciousness. The problem is that drugs leave you with no control over the state that you find yourself in. Even worse, they can lead to debilitating and destructive addictions and brain damage. I include alcohol as a mind-altering substance; I consider alcohol a drug.

There are those who argue that in some tribal cultures drugs were traditionally used to achieve altered states. While this is certainly true, it is also true that these cultures put those who used such mind-altering substances through rigorous training to give the user some control over the altered mental states. It was recognized that even a small error in judgment could bring about disastrous consequences, even to an experienced person. Part of the reason that many of these ancients used drugs to achieve altered states was that they didn't know any other way to do it. We can no longer use that excuse. With many street drugs and chemical hallucinogens, what is being touted as "altered realities" are merely the tricks your mind plays on you when your brain cells are being destroyed. There is no mystical import to chemically induced (and permanent) stupidity.

Since it is possible to achieve altered mental states without using such substances, I avoid the use of mind-altering drugs. In my opinion, the possible benefits are far outweighed by the risks involved. Warriors strive to maximize their potential. Drugs limit your potential. I have occasionally found myself in Circles where celebrants have showed up under the influence of alcohol or drugs. These individuals unbalanced the energy of the entire group, acting as an energy drain for the entire Circle. This is both inconsiderate and foolish.

If what you are trying to do is to face the challenges of life and take charge of your fate, using drugs is counterproductive. The Warrior strives to get more involved in his world and become the master of his situation. Using drugs removes you from the world and leaves you with no control. The addict tries to remove the stresses and difficulties in their life by using drugs to escape. The Warrior removes the difficulties and challenges of life by overcoming them.

Meditation for Effective Magick

Having said that, let's look at a number of meditation exercises that you can list in your Book of Shadows. These exercises will ultimately allow you to cultivate the focus of will needed for effective magick.

A trained person can meditate anywhere. An inexperienced person will find it easiest to start in a place that is relatively quiet and where you are not likely to be disturbed. It is probably best to start in a comfortable, seated posture. Later you can go on to doing these exercises standing in the Entering Tranquility posture that I described to you earlier. I often meditate in this posture in the middle of the police workout room. I've learned through practice to shut out the activity around me at will.

As can be seen from the Entering Tranquility posture described earlier, an upright posture is extremely important. It improves breathing and the flow of energy or chi. Sitting slumped over decreases the flow of oxygen. Eventually it will lead to distracting discomfort. If you are seated, you can use the same trick that we used in Entering Tranquility to achieve this. Imagine that a string is attached to the top of your head and is pulling you upward.

You will need something to focus your attention on. Since our natural perception is predominantly visual, we'll use visual exercises to start with. Later you can experiment with exercises involving the other senses of sound, smell, taste, and touch if you like. To begin with, I would strongly suggest using a visual object that moves. Movement captures our attention; advertisers often use action and motion in television commercials to capture our interest. Typical examples are:

- A candle flame
- The second hand of a watch
- A feather suspended from the ceiling on a string

Give yourself to the moment. Put expectations out of your mind in these exercises; accept what comes. You're learning to "listen" here. Many people seem to think that what should come out of meditation are images of happiness, light, and peace. You can direct your meditation this way if you wish; this is one of the ways to use meditation to heal. This isn't what we are seeking with the following exercises, however. You are learning to be more aware of what is happening around you. I am asking you to cultivate your awareness. The aspect of deity or yourself that you may connect with in these exercises may not be one of these "flowers and light" aspects on a given day. The main aspect of deity that I naturally connect with is the Morrighan. She certainly has a loving aspect, but many times she has a serious and weighty message to deliver to me.

Relax. If your body is tight or tense this will restrict the flow of chi and eventually cause distracting discomfort. Breathe naturally and deeply. Don't rely on shallow chest breathing; relax your abdomen and let the diaphragm drop, drawing air deep into the lungs. Focus on your breathing at first. Take a deep breath in, hold it a moment, inhale a little more, then exhale completely. Once you have exhaled, hold a moment, then exhale a little more before taking the next breath. After a while you will do this without thinking about it. Inhaling a little extra before exhaling and vice versa helps you to do this deep breathing with less discomfort. If you are distracted or preoccupied, imagine that your concerns are being expelled from you each time you exhale.

Once you are relaxed and your breathing is settled, try meditating on the object of your choice without thinking. The latest studies indicate that suppression of the twelve to twenty-four cycles per second beta waves in your brain allows your inner vision to unfold. What this means is that you are shutting down the left side of your brain to allow the right side to work more freely. It is hard to achieve a calm state of awareness if the brain is rushing along at twenty-four cycles a second.

Simply experience the object in front of you. Don't think about it. You want the impressions that come to you to originate in the intuitive part of you where they will arrive without conscious thought. Beginners often find that their undisciplined mind tends to wander. Don't try to force this process. Don't mentally kick yourself in the butt if you catch yourself going off on some train of thought or other. Just say to yourself "thinking," and start again. With practice, you will be able to focus on the object without thinking for longer and longer periods. The object here is to try to hold the object as long as possible without outside thoughts intruding. Eventually this will improve your concentration. The longer you can maintain an image in your mind, the greater the magickal effect (more on this later). Keep track of your progress and the duration of your meditation in your Book of Shadows.

Using Mandalas

Another useful meditation tool is mandalas. A mandala is a symbolic diagram. It is often round or oval in shape, though mandalas may come in square, triangular, or polygonal shapes as well. They may be relatively simple or enormously complex. Many are designed specifically for contemplation or meditation. Simpler designs are often referred to as *Yantras* (a Sanskrit word for "meditation sign").

You can use readymade mandalas drawn from any number of religious traditions in your meditation. You may also draw upon the store of symbols that you documented under "Dreams" in your Book of Shadows. The mandala is used as a focal point for your meditation. My favorite hangs in my office where I write. It is a circular design called "Keltic Mandala" that was created by Jen Delyth. It is a very elaborate Celtic knotwork design depicting the cycles of the seasons.

You use a mandala as a visual focal point for your meditation. Let your mind become still and then see what impressions the mandala brings into your mind. This is a useful technique if you find yourself blocked or stuck for ideas. Record these impressions in your Book of Shadows.

How much you meditate each day depends on your needs and your level of competence. It is a good practice to gradually work up from ten minutes a day to thirty minutes a day. Don't rush things. It usually takes up to a year to master basic meditation.

Once you have achieved some success with this meditation technique, try this variation: Try looking at the shadows of things rather than the objects themselves. For example, when viewing a tree in sunlight, most people look at the pattern of light as reflected by the leaves. Instead, try meditating on the patterns made by the shadows. This technique will train your mind to look at things more completely. It will teach you to look for the unexpected. Using shadows cast by natural sunlight is the best place to start; such shadows naturally move, which tends to hold the beginner's attention.

Next try focusing with your other senses. Close your eyes and listen to what is happening around you. Choose a sound and focus on it. I have a small pond with a waterfall in my backyard. I can sit in that garden and focus on the sound of the waterfall. Try to hold that sound in your mind to the exclusion of all others. You will probably surprise yourself with the number of sounds around you that you weren't aware of before.

If you have not meditated before, or have not done so for a long time, you will often experience a rush of unbidden thoughts, images, and sensations. This is caused by the release of built-up stress. People with few outlets for accumulated stress tend to store up this psychic garbage in their mind. Exercises like this give it an outlet, and it can all come rushing out suddenly. It can take the form of racing thoughts. Sometimes it takes the form of impressions of something or someone at the edge of our range of vision; you turn your head to look and there is nothing there. It can come on as unusual or unpleasant feelings, an odd smell, a voice. Sometimes the tension produces a headache. This is normal. Let it pass and start again. As the store of built-up energy diminishes, so will these "hypnogogic images" diminish.

If the impressions seem overwhelming, there is a simple technique that you can use to dispel them. Focus on the uneasy sensations. Imagine that they are a dark cloud within you. Out loud (or in your mind) shout out, "Haa! Haa! Haa!" With each shout imagine the cloud (and the sensations within it) being expelled from you. See the cloud receding into the distance until it vanishes from sight.

Becoming Sensitive to Energy

In chapter 6 I introduced you to the idea that you could receive energy, as well as send it, through your hands. Training your hands to be receptive is quite easy. Hopefully by now you will have done the exercises in chapter 6 and will have developed a feel for what the flow of chi through your body feels like. This will help you to recognize its flow in others.

First, try holding your hands over various parts of your body to sense the flow of energy under your skin. Later you can try this with a partner; try to locate "hot spots" that may indicate the presence of an injury or illness. Try locating each of the chakras that I described in chapter 6 with your hands. Sense the energy at each of these locations, starting at the bottom at Muladhara and working upward. You can often determine where an energy blockage is occurring using this technique. Once you have located the spot, you can use the same hand to reverse the flow and project healing energy into the site. Record your impressions and results in your Book of Shadows.

Try this sensitivity exercise with other living things. Try sensing the chi flowing in plants and trees. Sense the chi flowing through your dog or cat. Notice how your pets react to energy that you project. Animals are much more in tune with these subtle flows of energy than the average human in today's world. Record the results in your Book of Shadows.

Drawing Down

I have found that all of the world's religions have means of altering states of consciousness. Some religions use mind-altering substances to achieve this. An example of this is the use of peyote in the religion of the Southwest Native Indians. Even the Judeo-Christian religions have retained a substance for this purpose—alcohol. Wine is used in the Catholic ceremony of transubstantiation (consubstantiation if you're Protestant). Other religions use breathing techniques, chanting, drumming, and a variety of other techniques to achieve this end.

One of the common characteristics of religions is that these altered states often manifest as a possession by a mythological deity of the religion in question. For example, Christian Charismatics are "taken by the Holy Spirit" and speak in tongues, Spiritualists "channel" a spirit entity, and Christian Fundamentalists speak of the dangers of "demon possession." In Santería the Orisha (deity) is said to "ride" the celebrant, who is often referred to as a "horse." In Voudoun the same process occurs, the Loa, or *Mystere* (deity), taking possession of the celebrant. Great care is taken in Santería and similar religions to carefully choose the correct Orisha/Loa to dedicate the aspiring priest or priestess to, since this is the entity that will manifest itself in the priest or priestess from that point on.

Wicca has its equivalent of this process, which is called "Drawing Down." Wiccan Priestess Kate Slater once wrote:

> If you believe in a perceivable, transcendent Goddess or God or multiples of the same, then it follows logically that you can feel Her/Him enter you and let that voice speak. If you believe that the Sacred is always immanent within everything and doesn't have a human personified gender-attributed face (other than the way in which humans often choose to meet it through a face or aspect) then whose voice is speaking? Do

you have to be a Deist to do this? If you aren't, can you access
the sacred connection within yourself and give that to others,
either through an aspect that you understand something of,
such as the Crone, or directly? Is that also Drawing Down?[3]

All of us find ourselves looking at exactly the same thing out
there when we go looking for deity or spirituality. But because we
come from different educational, cultural, and social backgrounds,
we end up seeing different things. We are trying to describe the
indescribably immense. When we experience things for which we
have no previous frame of reference, we struggle to explain them in
terms of other frames of reference that we already possess.

Thus several different people may experience the same divine
revelation simultaneously, and yet one will see the Virgin Mary,
another Gaia, yet another Jesus, and still another a UFO. In the
East they call this phenomenon Maya, meaning "illusion." This
does not mean that what these people perceived does not exist, it
simply means that each person perceives what they see in a
uniquely individual way. This process affects what deities show up
in Drawing Down.

All religions have some form of changing a person's conscious
state; some have several. Each leads the participant to experience
deity in a particular way. In other words, the religion supplies terms
of reference with which the follower defines and, to a certain
extent, limits their experience of deity. Wicca is no exception, but in
Wicca much more flexibility is allowed in interpreting the experience of deity. We must strive to preserve this freedom of expression.
There is a tendency within organized religions for people to gather
into cliques, each insisting that their interpretation, their terms of
reference, are somehow superior. This is Maya, or illusion, and as
such is a poor basis for trying to establish your superiority.

The most common perception of deity within Western society is
that deities are individual entities, separate from their worshippers.

Divinity is considered to be separate from the mundane. As I pointed out earlier, Wiccans have a different perception; that divinity is inseparable from the mundane. I maintain that just because a person does not always have conscious access to deity, it does not necessarily mean that we are separated from the source of this information. It could simply be that you need to enter another state of consciousness to become aware of the connection, the source, or the insights that were there all along. I believe in this sense we are all continuous reflections of the Goddess or God. Of course, this is my perception of the situation, and I say this in full awareness of the principle of Maya I already mentioned.

There are two theories to explain what happens during the Drawing Down. The first is that the deity takes temporary control of the individual. The other possibility is that some aspect of the individual's personality is activated and manifests as one of these divine entities. If divinity is inseparable from us, then the difference is academic, as the end result is the same.

In Wicca, Drawing Down can take two forms:

◆ *Conscious Channeling*—The person Drawing Down is aware of what is happening to him and can recall what has occurred after the trance ceases.

◆ *Unconscious Channeling*—The person Drawing Down is unaware of what is happening to him and cannot recall what has occurred after the trance ceases.

I have personally experienced both forms. There are times in the past when I have entered such a state, aware of giving up control to some other intelligence and seeming to step back inside myself to experience the process. Other times I have blanked out and had to rely on other persons present to tell me what transpired afterward. Often as I entered the trance I felt myself lifting up. The next thing that I felt was a dropping down again into myself as the trance ended. It is a peculiar sensation; it felt as if I were stepping into a body that wasn't quite assembled right. Afterwards I sometimes feel disoriented and unsteady on my feet for a few moments.

I've noted a number of parallels when I compare the successful Drawing Downs that I have experienced to the "possessions" that occur in Santería or Voudoun:

> Each participant seems to have certain deities or aspects that appear each time they Draw Down. Rather than a different one appearing each time, the same entities seem to re-appear each time in that individual. This seems partially to be a function of which deities the individual has an affinity for. In Wicca there is usually no formal process to choose which deity will manifest. In Santería this is a very serious and complex process in which various forms of divination are used to determine the correct Orisha that the Santero or Santera is to dedicate themselves to. Although the Orishas may appear at any time in anybody, it is ordinarily the Orisha that the Santero or Santera is dedicated to that will appear in that Santero or Santera.

> The "Drawing Down" is done within the context of a ceremony in a ritual circle. In Santería the Orishas "ride" their followers within the context of a magickal ceremony too.

> In Wicca, the Drawing Down is usually done with an assistant or assistants that help the manifestation occur and help to sustain it. This usually takes the form of a person reciting certain ritual lines, welcoming the God and Goddess to come. In Santería it involves the Apkwon (ritual singer) who encourages or cajoles the Orishas to the accompaniment of drums (bata) until the Orishas appear. Once they do, the Apkwon welcomes, praises, and flatters them, to encourage them to stay.

> Some Wiccans use drums to produce a low "heartbeat" rhythm that seems to help the person Drawing Down to sustain the trance. Drums are used in Santería and related religions too, but to a much greater extent and in a much more formalized fashion.

Drawing Down may be carried out singly or in groups. This group practice is commonplace in Afro-Caribbean religions such as Santería, Macumbe, and Voudoun. Their reasoning is that the Orisha or Loa (deity) is too immense to be entirely contained within a single human being, so the Orisha lets only a tiny part of its essence inhabit the human being "ridden" (i.e., Drawing Down the particular aspect of deity). Thus the deity can parcel out many small parts of its essence to several persons simultaneously. Of course the ritual involved in this case is designed to allow for such group channelling, and the disadvantage is that the aspecting is a more haphazard event, affecting celebrants at random within the ritual site. Certainly the concept of Drawing Down, using a different technique to elicit a specific response in a particular individual, is more likely to produce a predictable outcome.

If everyone has the ability to access deity directly, why Draw Down at all? Why have someone else channel the deity for you? In fact, there is no reason that I can see for Wiccans not to communicate with deity directly. This does not necessarily have to involve channelling. I have used Tarot and various forms of skrying or trance to accomplish this for myself many times in the past. One of the great advantages of the Wiccan religion is that we can free ourselves from the structure of the Judeo-Christian-Islamic religions, in which a bureaucracy "dispenses" religion to lay followers. In Wicca we can all meet on an equal footing.

Unfortunately, Drawing Down can be abused by those who wish to masquerade as deities for their own purposes. People having such an agenda may insist upon maintaining such a system, as without it they will not have the opportunities they seek to exercise their influence over others. They may use this "mask" of deity to say things and do things to others that they haven't the nerve to say to them ordinarily. This is dishonest and unethical.

This is another way of creating a bureaucracy. There is no scripture, but the followers must rely on a select few to interpret the spiritual for them.

Others may insist upon maintaining this system by creating the impression that they are in possession of an exclusive skill. They can then turn channelling into a sort of business, like some of the New Age mediums do. Sometimes this becomes a means by which a person gratifies their ego, collecting followers around them like a guru. In this situation we once again see a self-serving bureaucracy taking form.

Given that there are so many possible abuses of Drawing Down, and given that we all may contact deity directly, why bother Drawing Down at all? One argument in favor of Drawing Down is that it is often difficult for a person to be objective when trying to do any form of divination for themselves. Having another Draw Down for you would provide an outside perspective, and remove any personal biases. Another argument for it is that it can be used to enhance a ritual drama, where the persons representing the various deities are channelling the aspects of these deities during the ritual. I have seen this done with spectacular results in years past at the recreation of the Eleusian mysteries at Spring Mysteries festival in Washington State. I have also experienced rituals at Dragonfest in Colorado in which several people simultaneously Draw Down different aspects of the Goddess or God, allowing participants to select the aspect that they wish to communicate with. A couple of my acquaintance, who use Roman mythology in their Circle, Draw Down the Goddess and God upon themselves during their rituals, but do not actually say anything. Instead they sit on "thrones" provided for this purpose, becoming living representatives of the deities presiding over the ritual, a sort of living symbol or icon, receiving the offerings in a manner similar to that practiced in the Afro-Caribbean religions.

Certainly Drawing Down, as practiced by followers of Wicca, calls for a high degree of honesty and professionalism on the part of the person performing it. Not only does the priestess or priest have to act in an impartial and ethical manner, but they have to be forthright and admit when they are not able to perform Drawing Down, as sometimes happens. They have to resist the pressure to "perform" and get on with other things. Drawing Down is a subject fraught with pitfalls for the unwary and unscrupulous, but it can be a very beneficial experience.

One final note of caution. If you decide to do Draw Down, there are some precautions you should take. The first is to clearly define the parameters of the experience. Exactly how long do you want to stay in this state? I know of several people who invited in aspects like Pan without specifying how long they intended him to stay. It was several months later when their lives were upside down that they suddenly realized that he hadn't actually left. Which brings us to the second tip. Always remember to ground out the energy afterward (more on this in chapter 10).

In this chapter you've learned about the second side of the Witch's Pyramid: *To Keep Silent.* You've added a new Warrior Precept to your list: *Perceive that which cannot be seen with the eye.* You've learned about awareness, patience, and satori. We've discussed the benefits of achieving altered states without drugs. You've added a number of meditation techniques to your Book of Shadows. Hopefully this will be making you more aware of the energetic currents around you. Next let's look at how you can use what you have learned so far to empower yourself.

Endnotes

1. Dan Millman. *The Way of the Peaceful Warrior,* p. 82.
2. Bruce Lee. (1975). *Tao of Jeet Kune Do,* p. 20.
3. Kate Slater. (1994). Position Paper on Drawing Down, "Hearing Voices," p. 2.

9

Empowerment

Power! Did you ever hear of men being asked whether other souls should have power or not? It is born in them. You may dam up the fountain of water, and make it a stagnant marsh, or you may let it run free and do its work; but you cannot say whether it shall be there; it is there. And it will act, if not openly for good, then covertly for evil; but it will act.

Olive Schreiner, *The Story of an African Farm*

ONE OF THE many reasons that many people get involved in Wicca is that they want to use magick to take control of their lives. That is probably one of the reasons that you purchased this work in the first place—you were looking for magickal power. I can hand you a book, but I can't just hand magickal power to you. True achievement of magickal power over your situation is something that you must achieve yourself. "Power can be taken, but not given. The process of the taking is empowerment in itself."[1]

The basis of many books of magick is a list of spells, hexes, and curses. This is what a typical Grimoire is, a "cookbook" or "instruction manual." The author attempts to anticipate all of the different contingencies that a person may need a magickal spell to correct. Just follow the instructions, recite a couplet, and cross your fingers. The problem with this approach is that it doesn't encourage the reader to learn the basics of magick. The magickian ends up mechanically doing things he doesn't understand. The results are bound to be hit and miss. As you have already seen in what you've read up to this point, true magick requires a lot of study and discipline.

Another problem with this "cookbook" approach is that it tends to treat the universe like a machine. All magickal power is treated as an external process. Supposedly, the cogs of the machine start turning when we use the right controlling actions or words. This is a Newtonian worldview, not a Wiccan one. As I have pointed out repeatedly in this work, magick is an internal process.

I'm not going to list a bunch of spells for every occasion here, but rather list a series of techniques you can adapt to your needs. I encourage you to be creative and imaginative. This is the Warrior's way. After a while you will develop your own style of magick.

The next step in this process of developing your magickal skill is to write down the ninth Warrior Precept in your Book of Shadows:

Ninth Warrior Precept

Power with.

Grimoires often require the magickian to dominate someone or something. This is a concept that Starhawk labeled "power over." This approach is not the Warrior's way. The Warrior's power is "power with." The Warrior's aim is to harmonize or entrain herself with the universe surrounding her, which all exists on one level, overlapping. As I pointed out earlier, you become the valve or gateway through which the energy flows.

Power with does not imply that one does not ever exert control over other people. As a police officer, I often have to exert my authority to control chaotic situations. But I only exert as much as is necessary to control a situation.

"Power over" leads people who seek mastery of magick to treat magickal power as an external process. They attempt to use ritual to control energies or entities outside of the Circle. They treat magickal power like chattel—something to possess. Neither the energy that I raise, nor the power that results from it, belongs to me or anyone else. We're all simply tapping in to the vast universe around us. Becoming more masterful isn't a matter of stockpiling power. For the Wiccan Warrior, mastery is a matter of learning to use the power available to everyone more effectively. Power isn't something you own, it is something you achieve. True magickal power comes from within you. Ralph Waldo Emerson told us that "what lies behind us and what lies before us are tiny matters compared to what which lies within us."[2] I want to you look inside of yourself and find that magickal power that is in each of us.

Warrior Names

Part of this process of empowering yourself is choosing a warrior name. Taking a Warrior name for yourself may seem to be a trivial step in reinventing yourself. Yet names can have great transformative powers. You'll recall that earlier I said that we create the deities that create us in return. Choosing a Warrior name is simply an extension of this process. Names reflect our perception of ourselves. They help shape what it is we intend to be. In many ancient societies, people were given a childhood name by their parents. When they became adults, they chose an adult name. In *The Complete Book of Magical Names,* Phoenix McFarland put it this way:

> The names we choose for ourselves can serve as magical tools as we travel on our individual paths. A name can be an inspiration (Venus, Athena, Phoenix); it can label us by our attributes (Quicksilver, Elder, Oak, Golden) . . . and can

inspire us to change. Our names can associate us with elemental powers and bring that energy into our lives (Ariel, Sundance, Cascade, Terra). A name can help to improve how we feel about ourselves (Willendorf, Gaia, Plato). It can emphasize where we are now or where we hope to go. It can make us feel more powerful, wiser, more beautiful, more commanding, gentler, stronger, more female/male, fertile, etc. There is no limit to what a name can bring into our lives, except for those limits we put on it ourselves.[3]

A Warrior name can be an inspiration to you. It helps you to mold your self-image to help you to become the person you want to be. This name represents the goals and dreams you are working toward. Every time you use it, you remind yourself of your objectives. This name is one of the tools you will use to create your own reality.

When I first dedicated myself to the Wiccan path, I was a timid young man with rather low self-esteem. I desperately wanted to become someone more powerful. I wanted more control over my situation. The secret name I first chose for myself was "Conan." I didn't know what the name meant, I just knew from my comics and fantasy novels that it was the name of a powerful Warrior. I remembered being embarrassed at the time for choosing such a name. I never told anyone that I had chosen this special name. I hardly resembled such a heroic figure at the time.

I know now that Conan means "high" or "lifted up." It was probably the idea encapsulated in that name that help drive me to achieve what I have today. Later I took another Warrior name inspired by another hero found in Celtic mythology—Cuchulain. This name I use publicly, but to me it still represents my spirit and my goals.

Prosperity and Achievement

The element of Earth does not just symbolize our perception of our worth as human beings. It also represents material worth, reward, and the treasures of the earth. Earth manifests prosperity.

We all dream of better things. Ambrose Bierce called the future "that period of time in which our affairs prosper, our friends are true and our happiness is assured."[4] It is a curious thing that so many Wiccans I meet dream of being prosperous and then do nothing to realize these dreams. You'd think that people who understood the intricacies of magick would know how to handle this problem. Yet so many Wiccans of my acquaintance buy a handful of lottery tickets, cross their fingers, and dream on.

Dreams do not become reality unless you pursue them. Pursuing dreams is what magick is all about. As I have pointed out several times up to this point, what it all comes down to is personal responsibility. Warriors are not victims; they create their own reality. Abandoning yourself to "fate" will not get you the prosperity you want. To become prosperous you must take charge of your life. This will require work on your part. So often I run into people who figure that magick should bring them instant gratification. Phyllis Curott once described it to me this way:

> This is a fertility religion. You plant the seed, you water it, you nurture it, you weed around it. Ultimately you harvest what you cultivated. That's how our magick works. And whatever you do, you don't pull on the plant to help it grow![5]

There seem to be quite a number of Wiccans out there who enable their poverty and lack of control over their lives by treating their condition as if it were in some way noble. They sneer and scoff at prosperous members of the community, while at the same time wishing that they had money to pay their bills.

What kind of person is the average millionaire? You may be surprised. Many of us operate under the misconception that all wealthy people are prodigious spenders who buy a lot of expensive toys. We have this Hollywood image of people who are pampered and wasteful. In reality, most millionaires live well below their means.[6] They wear inexpensive suits and drive average cars.[7] One Texan millionaire that Stanley and Danko interviewed in researching their book, *The Millionaire Next Door,* had this to say:

[My] business does not look pretty, I don't play the part . . .
don't act it. . . . When my British partners first met me, they
thought I was one of our truck drivers . . . They looked all
over my office, looked at everyone but me . . . I don't own big
hats, but I have a lot of cattle.[8]

In their study, Stanley and Danko identified seven common
factors of millionaires:

1.   They live well below their means.

2.   They allocate their time, energy, and money efficiently, in
     ways conducive to building wealth.

3.   They believe that financial independence is more important
     than displaying high social status.

4.   Their parents did not provide economic outpatient care.

5.   Their adult children are economically self-sufficient.

6.   They are proficient in targeting market opportunities.

7.   They chose the right occupation.[9]

I don't put my faith in lucky charms. I don't knock myself out
doing magick to improve my luck. I make things happen in my life.
I do magick to increase my fortunes. I make my own good fortune.

I use my magick and divination to help me find and take advantage of the opportunities I need to earn my living. I work hard and
use my magick to make me more effective. If unexpected bills
arrive, I write articles. I use my divination to find the right market
for them. I use my magick to help these articles sell. When I need
extra cash, my magick attracts the call-outs and overtime at the
police station where I work. I take advantage of karma; I get back
what I put into the universe. Like the Texan in the previous example, I aim for cattle, not chattel.

If you despise the wealthy, you will never achieve wealth. There is nothing wrong with being prosperous. The idea that money is the root of all evil is part of the baggage that we bring with us from the Judeo-Christian world. It is what you do with your wealth that counts (there is that concept of intent again). There are some wealthy people out there who do despicable things with their wealth, but there are as many who are philanthropists who are worthy of our admiration.

If you want to become more powerful and prosperous, you must reach out for it. It doesn't come easily, but it is well worth working for. This is a fertility religion that honors hard work and stewardship. Used responsibly, prosperity will bring happiness and freedom to both the community and the Warrior.

In this chapter we've examined aspects of reaching for personal power. We've learned to focus on the basics rather than on the trappings of magick. You've added a new Warrior Precept to your Book of Shadows: *Power with*. You've chosen a Warrior name to help empower yourself. I've discussed the realities of prosperity and achievement. You've learned that the best approach is to make your own luck. In the next chapter we'll discuss how to protect yourself against the misuse of power by others.

Endnotes

1. Gloria Steinem. (1978). "Far From the Opposite Shore," in *Ms.* (New York, July 1978 and July/Aug. 1982; repr. in *Outrageous Acts and Everyday Rebellions,* 1983).

2. Ralph Waldo Emerson. (1870). *Society and Solitude,* "Courage."

3. Phoenix McFarland. (1996). *The Complete Book of Magical Names,* p. 35.

4. Ambrose Bierce. (1881–1906). *The Devil's Dictionary.*

5. Phyllis Curott. (2000). Comments from a discussion with the author at Blessed Be and Merry Meet in D.C. (BBMMDC), 14 October 2000.

6. Thomas J. Stanley, Ph.D. and William D. Danko, Ph.D. (1996). *The Millionaire Next Door*, p. 9.

7. Ibid., p. 8.

8. Ibid.

9. Ibid., list taken from pp. 3–4.

10

The Shield, the Stone, and the Circle

Spirit borrows from matter the perceptions on which it feeds and restores them to matter in the form of movements which it has stamped with its own freedom.

Henri Bergson, "Matter and Memory"

THE MOST COMMON Wiccan symbol for Earth is the Pentacle. A Pentacle is a pentagram engraved within a round disk of wood, metal, ceramic, or glass. The Pentacle is a symbol of both the earth and of the Wiccan's understanding of the universe.

One of the earliest magickal uses of the various forms of the Pentacle has always been as a form of protection. Thus the Pentacle represents the Warrior's Shield. Earthworks were an early form of fortification against attack. Thus, it is the element of Earth that teaches us the ways of shielding and protection. The weapons of Earth are used to protect us.

Over the centuries, people have relied on armor to protect themselves. Personal body armor has developed over the centuries from the simple shield and helmet of ancient Warriors, to chain mail, to elaborate suits of plate armor worn by medieval men at arms, to flexible armor vests worn by modern police officers and soldiers. All armor offers the wearer a certain level of protection. Yet for every type of armor, there is some form of weapon designed to pierce it. Battlements can be breached, defenses infiltrated.

Amulets are another common form of self-protection. They work in much the same way as candle magick; they serve as a focus that repeatedly reminds us of their purpose. Many people use the Pentacle as a protective amulet. Like armor, however, amulets and charms can be overcome if you know how to do it. So before you learn anything about shielding and defenses, I need to teach you not to simply rely on shields alone for protection.

I am often contacted by people who want me to protect them against psychic attacks or negative energy. Often these people have consulted a legion of "occult experts" and healers before coming to me. They have spent a lot of time and money trying to get others to build up some sort of magickal defenses for them. Often these defenses, if they work at all, only work for a short time. They eventually erode as their energy is depleted, like a battery running down. It is preferable to develop your personal magickal skills to deal with situations like this instead of relying on others to apply "Band Aid" cures. Nowadays I rarely concern myself over negative energy or intent that people direct at me. I have developed my personal chi and will to the point where most of the negative stuff tossed in my direction bounces off without me even having to think about it.

When considering your safety, it is best to start with simple principles. Any safety-conscious cop will tell you that one of the most important safety principles is the elimination of habits and routine. Keep going to the same coffee shop every shift at the same time, and sooner or later somebody who wants to get you will figure this out and ambush you. A Warrior has no routines. A Warrior is, as Don Juan so aptly put it, "unavailable." The Warrior is spontaneous, fluid, and never a creature of habit. This is actually one of the lessons of the element of Air, and I will return to this idea later in the book. I wanted to mention this principle here to put into perspective the matters of shielding.

Part of creating your own reality is taking responsibility for habits that have become problems in your life. Habits are no accident. We make choices in life and some of them aren't that well thought out. Yet they are our choices. The shaman Agnes Whistling Elk once said:

> Every act has a meaning. Accident is a word born of confusion. It means we didn't understand ourselves enough to know why we did something.[1]

That is why I have emphasized the importance of self-knowledge in this work. Understanding why we have developed habits or addictions is one of the most important steps in overcoming these compulsive behaviors. I started this work with an examination of the Wiccan Rede, which began, "An it harm none . . ." "None" includes "you."

Few of us succeed in eradicating problem behaviors on the first try. Often such behaviors are ingrained and require persistence to overcome. The following verse by Portia Nelson admirably illustrates the common pattern that most of us go through in the process of overcoming a habit or addiction.

Autobiography in Five Short Chapters

1.
I walk down the street.
There is a deep hole in the sidewalk.
I fall in.
I am lost . . . I am helpless.
It isn't my fault.
It takes forever to find a way out.

2.
I walk down the same street.
There is a deep hole in the sidewalk.
I pretend I don't see it.
I fall in again.
I can't believe I am in the same place.
But it isn't my fault.
It still takes a long time to get out.

3.
I walk down the same street.
There is a deep hole in the sidewalk.
I see it's there.
I still fall in . . . it's a habit.
My eyes are open.
I know where I am.
It is my fault.
I get out immediately.

4.
I walk down the same street.
There is a deep hole in the sidewalk.
I walk around it.

5.
I walk down another street.[2]

Sometimes people put off doing things, thinking that by doing so they are delaying the necessity of making a decision. There is an old adage, "Not to decide . . . is to decide." The trouble with letting sleeping dogs lie is that after a while the room fills up with dogs. Eventually you trip over one of those sleeping dogs and fall flat on your face.

Sometimes our habits are dysfunctional strategies that we use to give ourselves the illusion that we are in control of our situation. We are reluctant to let go of these habits as this feels like we are losing control. Letting go of such habits may seem like a loss of power at first, but it will lead to even greater power.

Another common mistake made by beginners on the magickal paths is to use magick to bail themselves out of a situation that they let get out of hand through laziness or neglect. Patching a situation up this way doesn't take care of the underlying problems that caused the situation in the first place. It is far better to deal with the core issues and prevent future problems than to be constantly using magick to get yourself out of corners that you have painted yourself into.

Overcoming your weaknesses takes a lot of courage. This is one of the lessons of the element of Water (more on this later). A Warrior must access his inner reserves to defeat his personal demons and take charge of his life. Act the way you'd like to be, and soon you'll be the way you act.

Eliminating bad habits will go a long way toward enhancing your protection. It will give you a stronger base to work from. Having established this foundation, you can use a number of other techniques to further protect yourself.

Shielding and Mirroring

Occasionally people feel the need to protect themselves against negative influences. This isn't as common a problem as some people think. Paranoia can lead some people to start flinging magickal thunderbolts at all manner of imagined threats. This invariably causes even greater problems. The whole subject of "psychic protection" needs to be approached with caution.

If you believe that things will go wrong, they usually will. This is a negative way of creating your own reality. If you believe that someone has the power to do psychic damage to you, it will amplify their intent and often give them that ability.

A good example of this is the theatrical traditions surrounding Shakespeare's play *Macbeth*. Many stage performers believe that it is "jinxed." They won't even use the name "Macbeth" when referring to it. My wife and I were once called in to a local theater company to show them how to overcome this. What we primarily did was to teach them how to defuse this ticking time bomb of belief. The play went ahead without incident.

I am not telling you to ignore negative energy directed at you. Nor am I saying that it is not possible to harm another with magick. I am saying that if you do nothing but sit and dwell on it, you'll only make it worse. Such destructive magick often relies on fear to get an effective hold on you. If you don't fear it, it won't work as well. The difficulty is that many people have not yet learned the skills they need to deal with such a problem. Until they do, they won't have the confidence to pull this off. That is why I will teach you some simple techniques to keep you safe until you have sufficient power and confidence to do without (there are those "training wheels" again). Just because it is possible to overcome armor and defenses does not mean to say that you should not use some sort of protection. A police officer would be a fool these days to go out on patrol without his personal body armor. No matter how carefully you plan, you may have overlooked something. Armor reduces the possible consequences of these oversights.

The approach I'd like you to take on this issue is derived from martial arts such as Jujitsu and Aikido. In these disciplines, you use the attacker against himself. You redirect the energy thrown at you. We are all drawing energy from the same pool. If destructive energy is sent in your direction, just put it back in the pool. What follows are some techniques for you to list in your Book of Shadows that will do just that.

Circle Casting

In chapter 5, you learned how a Wiccan creates sacred space by casting a Circle. Circle-Casting is one of the most common uses of energy for a Wiccan. It is possible to put up a Circle without any ceremony involved. This is an extension of the exercises I just described to create "balls" of energy. The only difference is the size of the energetic "ball" and your position in relation to it. In the earlier energetic exercises I had you molding the energy in front of you. In this case you put yourself inside of the ball of energy. This is precisely what a Wiccan Circle is—a sphere of energy. The Circle is simply where the sphere intersects the surface on which it is set up. The Casting that most Wiccans use to create a Circle is just a ritualized version of this process.

Try using the "Holding the Ball" exercise you learned earlier to set up a Circle. It may be easier for you at first if you trace out the perimeter of the Circle on the ground around you. This will help you visualize how far to let the energy ball expand. Stand in the center of the Circle in Entering Tranquility posture, facing north. Raise your arms into the Holding the Ball posture, and let the ball of energy form between your outstretched arms. Once you have let the ball of energy form in front of you using this exercise, fling your arms out wide and let the ball expand out to the perimeter of the Circle, enclosing you within it.

One thing that you will notice if you have set the Circle up properly is that the temperature inside the Circle seems to increase. A useful exercise for beginners is using the receptive ability in your hands to locate this sphere once you have created it. Reach out and explore the boundaries of it. You should feel that same heat and tingling that you noticed when the chi was flowing. Push a little more energy out and see how far you can get it to expand.

To close down the Circle, stand in the middle with your arms spread wide. Imagine the energy sphere collapsing in on itself. Gather it in, encircling it with your arms as if bringing it in to the position in front of your chest once more. Absorb it into the Dantian energy center in your abdomen (behind and below the navel), pressing your hands over this area for a moment. Then take a moment to stand in Entering Tranquility posture. Breathe deeply a few times, letting the chi within you come back into balance. Record your impressions in your Book of Shadows. This will help you keep track of your progress.

What I have just described is the technical process of Circle-Casting. You can dress this up to turn it into a ritual performance, and most Wiccans do. Most Wiccans use either their ritual dagger (the Athame), a ritual Sword, or a Wand to cast the Circle. I will speak more of the psychology of this in chapter 20. For now let me just say that the Magickal Weapon that you choose to cast with is used to help focus the idea that you are separating yourself from the mundane world.

The ritual details of the Circle-Casting ceremony used by Wiccans vary from one Wiccan tradition to the next. Since ritual practice is such a vast subject, I intend to cover it in a future book. For the purposes of this one, let's look at the common elements of a typical Wiccan Circle-Casting Ceremony in order to see what their purpose is. I've already mentioned the general pattern earlier in this chapter.

After the Altar has been set up and the ritual space cleansed, the Casting begins with the various elements being taken around the Circle to help connect the Wiccans within to the elements without. The Wiccan Casting the Circle then calls upon the elemental energies of the four cardinal directions to help connect to these elemental energies and the aspects of deity appropriate to these quarters. You may use whatever words seem appropriate for this purpose. In many Wiccan traditions, these elemental energies are referred to as Guardians or Old Ones, though other traditions use the term Guardians to refer to the coveners who stand outside the Circle to manage energy levels and provide security. Chose the symbolism that works best for you.

I encourage you to use whatever words come from the heart to make these elemental connections at the cardinal points. The energy flows much easier when one is relaxed. If you are standing all tensed up in the east desperately trying to remember your lines for invoking the Guardians, you aren't going to connect with that energy. Reading the words off of a card or out of a book isn't much better; you are focussing on the page instead of reaching out to connect with the elemental energy.

Having connected to the energies of the cardinal points, the Circle-Casting itself takes place. To cast in this fashion, start at the east side of the Circle, the place of beginnings and the rising sun. Adopt the Entering Tranquility posture to loosen up the energy channels in your body. Take a moment to imagine that you are putting down roots to tap into that energy. Once you have established the connection, let the energy begin flowing out of you through your hand or the Magickal Weapon such as a Sword held in that hand, using the Weapon as a focusing device. Turn and go deosil (sunwise or clockwise) around the Circle. In your mind's eye, see the energy streaming out to form the perimeter of the circle. Imagine the perimeter starting to glow. When you return to the east, turn inward and take up a position in the middle of the Circle before the altar. Hold up your arms and imagine the Circle filling out and becoming a glowing sphere of energy surrounding you. This is the same sphere of energy you were creating with the earlier exercise.

As the Wiccan Casting goes around the perimeter of the Circle, they usually speak words indicating that this Circle is a magickal place separate from the mundane world in order to reinforce this idea in the minds of the participants. Use whatever words you wish to do this. Remember, the energy flows best if you are relaxed. It is better not to use any words at all than stumbling about trying to remember set lines.

To close the Circle, it is traditional to disconnect from the elemental energies by going around the Circle widdershins (counter-clockwise) to each of the five cardinal points in turn and speaking words of dismissal. You then take the Magickal Weapon that you used to cast the Circle and draw it across the perimeter of the Circle. As you do this, imagine the sphere of energy collapsing in on itself back into you. Take a moment to stand in Entering Tranquility to allow the energy within you to come back into balance.

This sphere of energy, which is the Circle, is not an impermeable structure. It isn't a solid barrier. Household pets and people can walk through it at will. If this happens, it may disrupt the energy of the Circle. This may cause some discomfort for the people within it. There are occasions when a person may need to exit or enter a Circle after it has been cast. The procedure for creating a portal through which you can pass without upsetting the balance of the rest of the Circle is commonly called "cutting a doorway."

You can cut a doorway anywhere around the perimeter of the Circle, but it is traditionally done in the northeast. Using your hand or the Magickal Weapon that you used to cast the Circle, outline an archway at the perimeter of the Circle. Imagine as you do so that the energy draws back around it so that it creates a portal. If you used a Magickal Weapon to do this, lay it on the ground across the threshold and step out of the Circle. When you re-enter, pick up the Magickal Weapon and retrace the archway in reverse. Imagine the portal closing in on itself and sealing once again.

Mirroring

One variation of this Circle-Casting technique that you can use for self-protection is called mirroring. You can use this technique to reflect negative energy away from yourself. To do this, we will use the technique that I just described in which you let a ball of energy expand outward to form a protective sphere around you. In this case you needn't let it go any further that the surface of your skin.

Picture yourself wearing armor. It doesn't matter what kind: medieval plate or mail, Japanese samurai armor, Kevlar, it doesn't matter. Picture this armor covering you completely. If you want to reflect ugly stuff away, imagine this armor as having a highly polished reflective surface. Any negative energy that is being thrown at you is reflected back to the source.

You can think of this mirroring technique as a sort of "karma accelerator"—if the source is a person, this is going to reinforce the law of karma and dump negative energy in his or her lap. At the same time, by approaching the problem in this way, you are adhering to the Wiccan Rede. You aren't doing anything to harm anyone else. If any harm results, it is because the source has brought it on themselves.

The downside of mirroring is that the person who is the source of negative energy may perceive the energy reflected back as an aggressive act on your part rather than the passive act that it is. This may motivate him to fling even more in your direction. It may also cause him to enlist other people to his cause. These additional people may cause problems for you outside of the magickal realm. The situation may escalate.

Shielding

Another similar technique you can use is shielding. In this case, imagine the surface of your armor as a sort of grid or cage that captures the incoming negative energy and grounds it into the earth. This is one of the ways of putting the energy back in the universal pool. Another way of thinking of it is as a filter protecting you from unwanted energy. Your will selects what passes through the shield. The advantage of this is that it does not reflect anything back to the source. The source is still subject to karma, but their perception of the event is that their efforts are having no effect. After a while, this is bound to discourage them.

If you take the shield down for any reason, prepare yourself for a sudden inrush of energy. Be prepared to ground out the surplus so that it doesn't build up inside of you and make you ill.

A variation of this technique can be used in situations where you wish to go unnoticed. In this case imagine that you are clad in a sort of camouflage clothing that completely covers you. The surface of these garments gradually takes on the pattern of your surroundings, like a chameleon. It will be as if you are transparent. The energy slides over and around you, and is dissipated.

Whatever you do, avoid any sort of magick designed to "bind" or otherwise hinder the person sending negative energy at you. There is an old adage: Whatever you bind, you're bound to. The last thing that you want to do is connect yourself to this negative energy. You don't need to dominate here, you just need to control your situation.

Protective Circle-Casting

Earlier I discussed how the Circle is a sacred space that we create to make ourselves feel more secure while practicing ritual and magick. The Circle can also be used as a form of protection, though the main purpose of the ritual Circle is keeping magickal energy in. The technique of Circle-Casting can also be used to put some form of mirroring or shielding to enclose a particular area. This is commonly done to isolate residences and ritual sites from negative energy.

You can put up a "bubble" of energy around any areas that you want to protect. This is simply an extension of the Circle-Casting and mirroring exercises. Instead of imagining a suit of armor, do the Circle-Casting, expanding the bubble to take in the entire area you want to protect. Imagine this bubble or wall has a reflective shielding. For as long as the Circle remains up, it will act as a protective barrier to those within.

As with a ritual Circle, this protective bubble is not impermeable and will allow people and pets to walk through it. Each time that someone passes through it, however, it will disrupt it. Over time this will degrade it and make it increasingly less effective. If you intend to leave this protective bubble up for extended periods, you will occasionally need to recharge it to keep it working properly. Record the results in your Book of Shadows. This will help you keep track of how often such a bubble needs recharging.

At major festivals the entire site is often set up as sacred protected space for the duration of the festivities. The larger the area, the harder it is for a person to include it all in their imagination when trying to visualize the Circle. One way to simplify this task is to take a walk around the perimeter of the area in order to fix the boundaries in your mind. One useful trick is to imagine that every time your left foot or your Staff strikes the ground, a column of white light erupts from the ground. Once you have completed your circuit of the grounds, move to a central location. Here you visualize all of these columns of white light that you have created. With your will, bring the tops of these columns together to form a sort of protective "cage." When the ceremonies are over, simply imagine the columns of light withdrawing into the earth.

Grounding

One of the lessons of Earth is grounding. Grounding has several applications in Wiccan practice, one of them being protection. One of the simplest ways to do this is to put a line of salt around the area to be protected. Salt acts as a natural barrier, grounding out negative influences that flow across it.

Another use for grounding in Wicca is to enhance well-being. After you have been doing energetic work or magick, it is possible to build up surplus energy in yourself. Some of the chakras can become blocked. Symptoms of this include:

- *Restlessness* or *agitation*. People with such built-up energy can appear rather manic.

- *Confusion* or *distraction*. You may find it hard to concentrate or process thoughts.

- *Dizziness* or *lightheadedness*.

Experienced Wiccans usually don't have this problem, because they have learned to use themselves as a channel or conductor of the energy, letting it all pass through without collecting or impeding it. However, everybody has "off" days when they don't feel 100 percent, and even an experienced person can have this surplus build-up of energy occur. If you find yourself feeling lightheaded, dizzy or unfocussed following magickal work, there are several things that you can do to alleviate the problem.

First of all, several things are built into the typical Wiccan ritual to allow the participants to ground excess energy. One is the ceremony of "Cakes and Wine" at the end of most Wiccan rituals; consuming food and beverages "grounds out" energy and returns a person to normal waking consciousness. Note that I don't use wine; I use nonalcoholic beverages like fruit juice. Alcohol is a drug (a depressant) that alters the mind. It does ground the energy, but I've seen far too many people use it too liberally and end up literally grounded (that is, flat on their faces). It also grounds the energy of the other people in the Circle. I restrict alcohol use to activities outside of the Circle. If you feel the need to use some sort of soporific to slow yourself down, try valerian tea (more on this in the Book of Water).

Another way to ground is to place your hands on the ground or imagine that you are putting down roots. Imagine the surplus energy returning to the earth from which it came through these imaginary roots. One of my favorite grounding techniques is going out and working in the garden. I find that touching the soil naturally "grounds out" my surplus energy and restores my balance.

You can use these same techniques to disconnect yourself from aspects of deity that you may have been channelling in Drawing Down. Just imagine the divine energy passing out of you and restoring you back to your normal state of inner balance.

Another use for grounding is to handle overwhelming emotions like excessive anger. Anger is a natural emotion. There is nothing wrong with anger unless you let it get control of you. Here are some techniques that you can use to ground out unwanted emotions such as anger.

Sometimes you will be called upon to help ground one of your colleagues in Circle. It is best to make sure that you have centered and grounded yourself before you attempt this. You may also want to use a shielding or mirroring technique to set up a protective screen around you and the person that you are grounding to prevent any further exterior energy from making a bad situation worse. Cutting this person off from the flow of surplus energy around them is a very important step. If you don't do this before grounding them, the energy will be pouring into them as fast as you draw it out. Now ground the person by talking them through the procedure. Let the excess energy pass into the earth through their feet. You may have them ground by holding a Staff and using this as a sort of lightning rod to let the excess chi ground into the earth (more on this in the Book of Fire). Having the person hold a stone with grounding properties such as hematite may also be useful. If you are experienced in the use of chi, you can use yourself as a lightning rod to ground another person. Don't try this unless you are competent at grounding yourself. If the person you are grounding has no magickal training, teach her how to set up a simple shield for herself before you leave her.

After performing such a grounding for another, it is a good idea to center yourself using a variation of the Entering Tranquility posture. Stand with your feet together, hands at your sides. As you inhale, sweep your arms out to your sides and up until your palms are facing one another over your head, about six inches apart. Exhale, bringing your hands down with the palms facing the sides or your body until your arms are once more at your side. As you do this, imagine that the chi streaming out of your palms is sweeping the negative energy downward out of you into the ground at your feet. Repeat this action three times. After the last "sweep," bring your hands up to waist level, palms upward, and briefly clench your fists. Then let your arms hang down at your sides and let the chi within you balance out. This clenching action helps turn off the flow of chi from your palms.

Once you have developed your mastery of the magickal techniques in this book, you will be able to use your will to cancel out the negative influences thrown in your direction. Your intent will overcome any negative intentions directed at you. You'll do this almost automatically, without having to resort to casting circles or setting up defenses.

In this chapter we have examined the symbolism of the Pentacle. You've learned about eliminating habits and obsessions. We've examined psychic defenses such as mirroring and shielding. You've learned techniques of Circle-Casting and grounding. There remains one more aspect of Earth to examine—the seasons and magick of Earth.

Endnotes

1. Agnes Whistling Elk. *Medicine Woman* (as quoted by Amber K in *True Magick: A Beginner's Guide*, p. 66).
2. Portia Nelson. (1977). *There's a Hole in My Sidewalk*.

11

The Magick and Seasons of Earth

Winter is icummen in,
Lhude sing Goddamm,
Raineth drop and staineth slop,
And how the wind doth ramm!
Sing: Goddamm.

Ezra Pound, "Ancient Music"

PART OF THE energy I have had you draw upon up until now has been the energy of the earth under your feet. I have also had you ground excess energy into the earth. We should now look a little closer at what energy is encapsulated in, and how it can be focussed with parts of the earth itself.

The study of this energetic aspect of the element of Earth can be found in many traditions. On a grand scale, this is mirrored by magickal arts such as Feng Shui, in which your environment is set up to maximize the effectiveness of the chi surrounding you. In Western magickal work, the equivalent is the study of ley lines and places of power. In either case the intent is to seek ways to take this natural energy and bend it to our will. This is all part of the magick of the element of Earth.

Crystals

On a small scale, chi can be manipulated through the use of crystals or gems. In Feng Shui, the placement of crystals is often used to redirect, collect, or refocus chi. Crystals are placed in order to draw chi into locations where the energy is low. In First Nations beliefs, gems and stones were used for healing, protective and skrying properties. Many New Age traditions use them for skrying or to redirect or collect energy for various purposes. The Wiccan Warrior can use these crystals as focusing tools as well. Crystals can be used as extensions of yourself and your energy.

To do this, you needn't memorize the specific characteristics of minerals such as quartz or malachite. I've seen many conflicting lists published over the years. Different people seem to have different affinities to various minerals and gems. It seems that many of these characteristics of gems are primarily connected to the color of the substance. This makes sense, since the color is directly related to the wavelength of light energy being perceived. In other words, what is more important to you is the color of the stone and what it represents to you.

The following is a list of attributes normally associated with the various colors. Record this list of color attributes in your Book of Shadows. It will serve as a useful reference in your magickal work. You will use it in other forms of magick such as candle magick and cord magick later in this work.

White—Purity, spirituality

Red—Health, energy, strength, sexual potency, courage

Pink—Love, affection, romance

Yellow—Intellect, imagination, creativity, mental abilities, charm, confidence, persuasion

Green—Abundance, fertility, good fortune

Blue—Truth, inspiration, wisdom, protection, understanding, health

Purple—Financial success, power, idealism

Gold—Solar energy, male divinity

Silver—Lunar energy, female divinity

You needn't spend a lot of money at a lapidary shop or occult supply store to obtain crystals, though this can save you a lot of time and work. Stream beds and rock falls are wonderful places to find crystals to use and you don't have to spend a fortune to obtain them (this is, after all, where the shops get them). Meditating with these crystals will help give you a feel for what effects they have on you and your surroundings. Experiment with different types and record the results in your Book of Shadows.

The size of the stone is not as important as the use you put it to. You want to use this crystal tool as a lens to focus energy or store energy. Later in the book I will show you how to use the Weapons of Fire and Air to focus energy. The same techniques can be applied to crystals.

The difference between these crystals and the Magickal Weapons I just mentioned is that crystals have the ability to passively accumulate or redirect energy into your environment. If you are lacking certain things in your life, you can use crystals to attract them. This is the basis for their use in Feng Shui. These·crystals continue to work passively until you take them up in your hand and direct this energy where you will.

Once again, let me caution you not to place too much emphasis on paraphernalia such as crystals in your magickal practice. Stuffing crystals into your purse, your glove box, your desk drawers, and under your pillow will just tangle up the energetic currents and complicate things. In Feng Shui, a crystal or two is placed in strategic locations to achieve a certain effect. More is not better.

Stone Magick

There are other simple magickal uses for common stones as well. For example, if anger threatens to overwhelm you, find yourself a rock. Pour all of your anger into this stone. Once you have done this, throw it away from you (but not at the person you are angry with!). Imagine that the rock is carrying away your anger. I find that this is especially effective if I pitch the rock into the ocean. A variation on this is to take this rock and bury it deep in the ground. Some people carry a few "worry pebbles" around with them for this purpose. Whatever you do, don't keep the rock in your home or your pocket afterward.

Another variation of this technique is to charge a stone with energy to release later. These are traditionally called lightning stones or divinity stones. For example, you might charge a stone with healing energy and send it to a sick friend so that they can absorb it when they hold it. Of course the amount of energy that you can put into the stone is limited. It is far more effective to deliver this energy in person.

A stone may also be used to help a person ground-out surplus energy. Some people seem to find it easier to send such energy into a stone that they are holding than into the ground through their feet. Once you have grounded yourself, place the rock that you have used in water or on the ground outside to let it disperse the accumulated chi into the earth.

Seasons of Earth

Part of the energy and inspiration that the Wiccan Warrior can draw on is the power of the turning seasons. The seasons of Earth are the seasons of harvest and winter. This is the time of year when the crops are brought in and processed to preserve them for the winter seasons ahead. In ancient times, after the harvest seasons, the Warriors withdrew to their winter quarters. Precipitation, cold, and mud made it next to impossible to mount any kind of offensive actions. It was a time to heal the wounds acquired in the campaigning season. It was a time to repair weapons, burnish skills, and plan for the campaigning season ahead. It was a time to cull the herds, cure the meat, and tighten one's belt. The seasons of earth are seasons of preparation and planning.

Even in our modern society the seasons of earth affect us. For example, inclement weather in the seasons of Earth forces us to go inside to exercise. This is when people go to the gym to tone themselves up for the coming spring when they can take their activities outside.

Two Sabbats occur in this season of the element of Earth. The first is Samhain (pronounced "sow-in"), which occurs October 31. This is the Wiccan New Year's celebration. Samhain is the time of year that I make decisions about the upcoming year. Samhain is when I commit myself to resolutions and objectives for the next cycle of the seasons—these are my New Year's resolutions. As martial arts master Wong Kiew Kit puts it, "Having a clear idea of our aims and objectives, and reassessing our progress periodically, is imperative if we wish to achieve maximum results in minimum time."[1] My objectives are based on the review of my actions and accomplishments that I conducted in the preceding Seasons of Water (more on this in the Book of Water that follows). These are major objectives and resolutions; I often set lesser objectives as the need arises at other times of the year.

For example, at Samhain I determine the minimum number of books and articles that I intend to produce in the coming 12 months. Later, in chapter 18, I will speak about setting objectives in more detail. It is a good idea to record your objectives and goals in your Book of Shadows; this will reinforce them in your mind. You might even post this list in a prominent location to help motivate you. Making records of this sort allows you to check back from time-to-time to monitor your progress.

Samhain is traditionally a time when divination is done to help chart out your path in the coming year. There are a number of divinatory customs associated with Samhain (see the glossary, page 243). I won't go into the practice of modern methods of divination in this chapter. I will discuss the process of divination later in chapter 13. For now let me encourage you to use divination to help you determine the coming influences in your life. This will help you plan courses of action to deal with them.

Samhain is also the time of year when the veils between our world and the Summerland become thin. It is a time to remember ancestors and dear departed family members. It is a time to communicate with them to see if they have any wisdom to impart to us. Their achievements can inspire ours. Of course, not all of my ancestors were noble or wise, but learning about them I can learn their mistakes and seek to avoid them in my life.

The Lesser Sabbat that follows Samhain is Yule, which is the winter solstice. The Yule Sabbat is when I finalize the plans and strategies that I need to make the resolutions that I made at Samhain a reality. This is when I make the preparations necessary to achieve the objectives that I have set for myself.

Yule is traditionally a time to cleanse the household in preparation for the return of the sun. As the light begins to increase, so do your plans begin to grow and take shape. In the glossary I list some of the Yule customs that I practice in my household. This is when I use my magick to "clear the decks" for action.

The Yule season is the time of year when I finalize the lists of things I need, and things to do, for in the coming seasons I must get down to working toward these objectives. You must turn your list of objectives into a more detailed "to do" list, which outlines all of the steps that you need to carry out to achieve your objectives. This is the time to lay down the magickal foundations for what you hope to accomplish in the coming cycle of seasons.

Planning is one of the most important activities that a Warrior can engage in. Benjamin Franklin emphasized the importance of planning when he wrote:

> I have always thought that one man of tolerable abilities may work great changes, and accomplish great affairs among mankind, if he first forms a good plan, and, cutting off all amusements or other employments that would divert his attention, make the execution of that same plan his sole study and business.[2]

To achieve your objectives it will be necessary for you to exhibit a certain amount of daring. No human enterprise is entirely without risk. Therefore it is now time to move on to the next book in this work, the Book of Water.

Endnotes

1. Wong Kiew Kit. (1997). *Chi Kung: For Health & Vitality*, p. 17.
2. Benjamin Franklin. (1771–90). *Autobiography*, ch. 7 (published 1868).

Book Three

THE BOOK OF WATER

I T IS SAID that all life came from the primeval waters. Water is a fluid without shape, changeable and elusive. From the element of Water the Wiccan Warrior learns flexibility and adaptability. The element of Water also teaches us of the depth of human emotions, intuition, and psychic abilities. "Still waters run deep." Water is a universal symbol of cleansing and purification. It is also a symbol of regeneration. All over the world one finds springs, wells, and bodies of water with healing powers. The Celts believed that sacred springs and wells were connections to the otherworld. Water is a feminine element, linked to the tides and the moon. In the Wiccan's Circle the element of Water is found in the west. Undines are the spirits of Water. The color of the element of Water is blue, symbolizing deep waters.

The most beautiful emotion we can experience is the mystical. It is the power of all true art and science. He to whom this emotion is a stranger, who can no longer wonder and stand rapt in awe, is as good as dead. To know that what is impenetrable to us really exists, manifesting itself as the highest wisdom and the most radiant beauty, which our dull faculties can comprehend only in their most primitive forms—this knowledge, this feeling, is at the center of true religiousness. In this sense, and in this sense only, I belong to the rank of devoutly religious men.

Albert Einstein

12

To Dare

We must put [the knowledge] *into practice* [physically and mentally]. *What will be gained with mere words?*

Shantideva

THE ELEMENT OF Water is related to our emotions. The practice of magick demands emotional intensity. To make magick work you must have a passionate desire to attain your goals. I'm talking about gut feelings and yearnings here; intense feelings that make you shout out loud. "You must break through your conditioning, find the flame in your heart and the fire in your belly, if you are to change yourself and your world."[1]

Some books relate certain emotions such as passion to the element of Fire and to the south. I prefer to group all emotions under the element of Water. In my view the element of Water teaches us of the depth of human emotions, intuition, and psychic abilities. The element of water is related to the third side of the Witch's Pyramid: *To Dare.*

This side of the Witch's Pyramid is one of the two sides concerned with sending out magickal energy (the other being *To Will*).

You will recall in the Book of Earth I told you that another of the sides of the Witch's Pyramid, *To Keep Silent,* was one of the two grail processes of letting the energy or chi fill you. Yet here we are in the Book of Water where one of the Magickal Weapons is a Chalice, or grail cup, and I'm talking of sending energy out.

Let me assure you, there is no contradiction. I cautioned earlier about depleting your personal energy reserves by relying on your body alone as a source of magickal energy. That is one of the reasons you learned techniques for filling yourself with energy at the beginning of the book. Once you have filled that grail cup (which is yourself), you need to get the energy out of it so that you can direct it to your magickal objective. *To Dare* is the side of the Witch's Pyramid that allows us to do just that. Remember the principle I spoke of earlier in the Book of Spirit, "Chi follows I (energy follows intent)"? I will have more to say about intent in the Book of Air, but for now let me say that daring and intent go hand-in-hand. Think of daring as supplying the magickal pressure that forces the energy out of you toward your objective. First you learned how to build up the chi within you. Now I'm going to start showing you how build up the internal magickal "pressure" to send it out of yourself.

This is why it is important for us to begin this Book of Water with an examination of daring and courage and how this relates to the practice of magick. This leads us to the Tenth Warrior Precept to write in your Book of Shadows. Some of you with military backgrounds will recognize it as the motto of the British SAS (Special Air Service) Regiment.

Tenth Warrior Precept

Who dares wins.

To dare is to do what thou wilt. To dare is to have faith in yourself and your abilities, to let go of your inhibitions and doubts. Magick simply does not work for you if you don't believe that it will. As you hone your skills with practice, your experience and confidence will grow, allowing you to push yourself further than before.

My wife Phoenix once told me that she had great success in manifesting her desires when she was a novice practicing magick. That is, until she met someone who told her that they were very happy that almost half their spells worked. It never occurred to Phoenix that it might not work. After that, she had a much harder time getting results from her magick spells. "As soon as my doubt was kindled, I couldn't stop the blaze," she says.

If you do not trust in your magickal power, its strength and energy will be weakened. Belief gives your magick a firm foundation; it will make your magick more effective.

Confucius once said that only the supremely wise and the ignorant do not alter. Life is change, and many people let this process of metamorphosis take them where it will. One day they wake up and look in the mirror and don't recognize the person looking back.

It doesn't have to be this way. You can take charge of your life and make the changes in your life intentional. This is the Warrior's path I described in my previous book *Wiccan Warrior*. I strive to create changes in my life in conformity with my will. Yet many people are afraid to take this responsibility. They want to have some control over their situation, but they are afraid that they may fail in the attempt.

You have everything that you need within you to succeed on this path at this moment. All you need is the courage to go looking within for what you need. This is another aspect of personal responsibility. Thus, the eleventh Warrior Precept is:

Eleventh Warrior Precept

The Gods cannot help those who will not help themselves.

There is an old saying, "The two hardest things to handle in life are success and failure." Achieving your objectives will likely take a lot of hard work; anything worth achieving usually does. Attaining mastery of any enterprise usually involves failure at some point. You may fail along the way more than once before you achieve what you've set out to accomplish. Some people find failure devastating.

Failure is a vital part of the learning process. You won't learn if you never fail and you'll never fail if you don't try. As Irish dramatist Samuel Beckett so aptly put it, "Ever tried. Ever failed. No matter. Try again. Fail better."[2] Anything worth striving for involves taking risks. If you never try, you're never going to fail, but you're never going to succeed unless you try either.

Mistakes are an important part of the growth process, because hopefully you will learn from them. Failure is feedback. Sometimes you will make a mistake more than once before you master a particular lesson. This does not mean you are stupid. Keep in mind that persistence is a Warrior attribute. Persevere and you will overcome. "Patience and tenacity of purpose are worth more than twice their weight of cleverness."[3]

This is especially true of self-mastery. Self-mastery requires self-discipline and determination. Dan Millman's teacher Socrates gave him this advice, "Urges do not matter; actions do. Persist as a Warrior."[4] Learn to know the difference between persistence and entanglement. As I told you earlier, once you master yourself, all of your other problems out there take care of themselves.

I had a dream. I wanted to be a writer when I retired from police work. After studying the situation, I came to the conclusion that the most sensible approach would be to start writing immediately. I was determined to succeed. I wanted to work at my writing so that by the time that I retired it would be developed to the point where I was successful. I soon discovered, as many beginning writers do, that rejection letters are a fact of life, especially when you are learning the craft of writing. Such letters were definitely disappointing, to say the least. They discouraged me. Nevertheless, I examined the work that the publishers had rejected and started afresh. I took courses to polish my craft. I put aside several hours a day in my busy schedule to write. It took time, but I have succeeded sooner than I had originally anticipated. I now have several books published and write articles that are regularly published in several magazines. Persistence pays off.

Every successful person has failed at some point, some more than others. When you fail from time-to-time, keep in mind the following examples of successful people who have "failed":

- R. H. Macy failed seven times before his store in New York caught on.

- English novelist John Creasey received 753 rejection slips, but went on to publish 564 books.

- Babe Ruth struck out 1,330 times—the world's record—but he also hit 714 home runs.

- An MGM memo on the first screen test of Fred Astaire said, "Can't act! Slightly bald! Can dance a little!" Astaire kept that memo over the fireplace in his home.

- Ludwig van Beethoven's violin teacher called him hopeless as a composer.

- Enrico Caruso's teacher said he had no voice at all and could not sing.

- Walt Disney was fired by a newspaper editor for lack of ideas. He also went bankrupt several times before he built Disneyland.

- Thomas Edison's teachers said he was too stupid to learn anything.

- Albert Einstein did not speak until he was four and didn't read until he was seven. He was expelled from school for being mentally slow, unsociable, and a dreamer.

- Leo Tolstoy flunked out of college.

- Henry Ford failed and went broke five times before his success.

An old adage says, "Winners have a way—losers have a reason." Like the previous famous people, you will need to dig down deep at times to find the courage to overcome the obstacles you will encounter in life. Courage is not an absence of fear. Only the fool does not fear. As Mark Twain wrote:

> Courage is resistance to fear, mastery of fear—not absence of fear. Except a creature be part coward it is not a compliment to say it is brave; it is merely a loose application of the word. Consider the flea!—incomparably the bravest of all the creatures of God, if ignorance of fear were courage.[5]

Fear is something that cannot be avoided. You will face challenges of various sorts throughout your life. The greater the objective that you set yourself, the greater the fears that you are likely to face. Fear is a part of life.

You may not consider yourself heroic. You may be saying to yourself right now, "Oh, sure! Easy for him to say. He's a cop. He's doing dangerous stuff all the time." Being a cop, however, has given me the opportunity to see people in various walks of life facing any number of challenges. This has afforded me the privilege of seeing many unsung heroes. You may think that you live an ordinary life devoid of any kind of courage. I suggest to you that some of the finest examples of courage are the unsung acts of simple heroism that go for the most part unnoticed in people's lives. Presidential speech writer Peggy Noonan puts it this way:

Most people aren't appreciated enough, and the bravest things we do in our lives are usually known only to ourselves. No one throws ticker tape on the man who chose to be faithful to his wife, on the lawyer who didn't take the drug money, or the daughter who held her tongue again and again. All this anonymous heroism.[6]

I'm not talking about martyrdom or renunciation here. That is the shadow side of the Warrior. You may have to endure some hardship on your way to achievement, but if the suffering continues unabated you are likely missing a lesson you needed to learn. It is a sign of immobility and stagnation. If you are a perpetual victim, you are very likely allowing yourself to be one. Deliberately making yourself a martyr is not courageous. This is not the action of a Warrior. The idea is to take charge of the change in your life and create a reality you desire. Not many people desire unending heartache.

It helps a great deal if you have friends and family who will support you through the difficult stretches. Encouragement is a blessing when it can be had. Sometimes you will find yourself faced with situations where support is noticeably lacking, however. I mentioned earlier that it was my father's fondest dream that I should have had a military career as a pilot. For a time I pursued this career, thinking that it was what I wanted, too. In fact, it was a family tradition. Eventually I discovered that it wasn't my dream at all. I finally decided to leave the armed forces and start a career as a police officer. At about the same time, my father discovered that I was a Wiccan. My father had other plans for me in this area, too.

I certainly did not get much support from my family. I'm sure that they perceived me as a failure back then. There is an old Chinese proverb that seemed to apply to my situation then: Everyone pushes a falling fence. It was a difficult decision and a difficult time for me. For years I had nightmares about it. Yet I knew that

I'd never be happy unless I threw everything I had done up to that point away and started fresh. That was twenty-four years ago and I've never looked back.

Courage is overcoming the fear of failure. Nathaniel Hawthorne once wrote that "the greatest obstacle to being heroic is the doubt whether one may not be going to prove oneself a fool; the truest heroism is to resist the doubt; and the profoundest wisdom, to know when it ought to be resisted, and when it be obeyed."[7] To dare is to have faith in yourself and your abilities, to let go of your inhibitions and doubts. Philosopher Francis Bacon wrote, "If a man will begin with certainties, he shall end in doubts, but if he will be content to begin with doubts, he shall end in certainties."[8]

As you hone your skills with practice, your experience and confidence will grow, allowing you to push yourself further than before. You will discover those hidden reserves that we all have within us. We usually don't find these reserves until circumstances force us to seek them. Only when we are thrown out of the everyday routine into a crisis do we find out what we are really capable of.

In many books on the art of being a Warrior, the awareness of death plays an important role. All of us suffer from a fatal disease—birth. We are all going to die. You haven't time to waste, to doubt, or to procrastinate. The Warrior makes every moment count. He faces each challenge as if it is a life or death struggle. Nothing is unimportant. This is the spirit of daring that I'm talking about here. Don Juan Matus told his student Carlos:

> Use [the knowledge of your death]. Focus your attention on the link between you and your death . . . on the fact you don't have time and let your acts flow accordingly. Let each of your acts be your last battle on earth. Only under those conditions will your acts have their rightful power . . . It isn't [so terrible to be a timid man] if you are going to be immortal, but if you are going to die there is no time for timidity . . . Most people move from act to act without any struggle or thought. A

hunter, on the contrary, assesses every act; and since he has an intimate knowledge of his death, he proceeds judiciously, as if every act were his last battle. Only a fool would fail to notice the advantage a hunter has over his fellow men. A hunter gives his last battle its due respect. It's only natural that his last act on earth should be the best of himself.[9]

Buddhist monks sometimes meditate in cemeteries to remind themselves how frail their body ultimately is. You don't have time to be timid in this life. You should not waste any part of this gift that the Gods have given you. You aren't here to repeat the mistakes that you made in past lives. You are here to improve your lot in life. Consider the words of Czech President Václav Havel:

A human action becomes genuinely important when it springs from the soil of a clear-sighted awareness of the temporality and the ephemerality of everything human. It is only this awareness that can breathe any greatness into an action.[10]

By deciding to transform yourself from what you are now by following this Warrior path, you are undergoing a "little death." A death of what you were in order that you may be reborn as something better. This is the only form of sacrifice that Wiccans practice—self-sacrifice. We give up our old selves in order to find a greater self.

Don't hold back. The sky is the limit. Once you've made the decision to do magick, throw yourself into it heart and soul. Remember the words of British playwright J. M. Barrie, "We are all failures—at least, the best of us are."[11] Remember the battle cry of the Templars: "Be glorious!"

In this chapter we discussed the third side of the Witch's Pyramid: *To Dare*. We added two new Warrior Precepts to our book of Shadows: (1) *Who dares wins;* and (2) *The Gods cannot help those who cannot help themselves.* We talked about taking charge of your life and overcoming failures. You learned about persistence and courage. In the next chapter we will examine another aspect of magick that daring can enhance—divination.

Endnotes

1. Amber K. (1990). *True Magick: A Beginner's Guide,* p. 109.

2. Samuel Beckett. (1984). *Worstward Ho.*

3. Thomas Henry Huxley. (1870). "On Medical Education" address at University College, London (published in *Collected Essays,* vol. 3, 1893).

4. Dan Millman. (1984). *Way of the Peaceful Warrior: A Book That Changes Lives,* p. 136.

5. Mark Twain. (1894). *Pudd'nhead Wilson's Calendar,* ch 12.

6. Peggy Noonan. (1990). *What I Saw at the Revolution.*

7. Nathaniel Hawthorne. (1852). *The Blithedale Romance,* ch 2.

8. Francis Bacon. (1605). *The Advancement of Learning,* bk. 1, ch. 5.

9. Carlos Castaneda. (1974). *Journey to Ixtlan,* pp. 84-85.

10. Václav Havel. (1986; tr. 1990). *Disturbing the Peace,* ch. 3.

11. J. M. Barrie. (May 3, 1922). Rectorial address at St. Andrew's University, Scotland.

13

The Cauldron
and the Chalice

An absolute can only be given in an intuition, while all the rest has to do with analysis. We call intuition here the sympathy by which one is transported into the interior of an object in order to coincide with what there is unique and consequently inexpressible in it. Analysis, on the contrary, is the operation which reduces the object to elements already known.

Henri Bergson, "Introduction to Metaphysics"

THE MAGICKAL WEAPONS of Water are the Chalice and the Cauldron. The Cauldron is an ancient symbol of the Celtic Goddess Cerridwen or the Celtic God Dagda. To the Celts the Cauldron was an ancient symbol of rebirth, nurturing, and regeneration. Many ancient Celtic myths refer to the Cauldron as a sort of cornucopia that contains whatever food a person desires, and which is never empty. For example, the Dagda's Cauldron, named "the undry" or Uinde ("act of beholding") was never empty of food.

The "Cauldron of Rebirth" is another common theme in Celtic myth. A slain Warrior cast into the Cauldron of Bran the Blessed would come out again alive. It may have occurred to you that what you are doing to yourself here is casting yourself into the Cauldron to be reborn. You are re-inventing yourself as a more powerful magickal person. Performing magick is a creative process. Harold Rosenberg once said that "whoever undertakes to create soon finds himself engaged in creating himself. Self-transformation and the transformation of others have constituted the radical interest of our century, whether in painting, psychiatry, or political action."[1]

You may wonder why I would list an implement like a Cauldron or a Chalice as a Magickal Weapon. The reason is that the element of Water is associated with divination. Anyone who has served in the military or in law enforcement will see the connection here; military leaders and police officers can tell you how important it is to gather information or intelligence. Divination is simply an extension of the cultivation of awareness that we were speaking about in chapter 8. This heightened awareness allows the Wiccan Warrior to be ready to seize the opportunities that come, and to follow the path down which intuition leads him.

For example, for twenty-four years I have known police officers who act upon what they call "hunches," "instincts," or "gut feelings." Even though they often get results, they are usually loath to admit that they rely on such intuitive feelings, even to their close friends. Henry David Thoreau noted this in his *Journals,* "What is peculiar in the life of a man consists not in his obedience, but his opposition, to his instincts. In one direction or another he strives to live a supernatural life."[2]

Wiccans should actively cultivate their "intuitions" and put them to use. My use of these intuitive talents at work has earned me the nickname of "the Wizard." Yet there is nothing mysterious about it. You simply let yourself "listen" (which you will recall is another side of the Witch's Pyramid). You become more aware of the currents surrounding you. This awareness leads to comprehension, and you act on it.

A decade ago, Phoenix and I went up over 12,000 feet into the mountains near Fairplay, Colorado, to find her brother's property. Phoenix's father was buried there and she wanted to visit the site. I'd never been there before. On the way up the gravel road we went past the property without finding it. At the end of the road we turned around and came back down. I suddenly had an urge and did a U-turn. It felt like the right place to turn but I didn't understand why. We went back to the end of the road. Here we stopped and did a brief ritual in a natural Circle with a rock slab as an altar. Afterward, on the way back down, I got an uncontrollable urge to stop and take off my jacket in the same spot as the earlier U-turn. I still didn't make the connection. Laurel opened her door to pour out some coffee that was cold and recognized landmarks for her brother's property beside us at the side of the road. This is what I had been sensing all along. All you have to do is listen and trust in your abilities.

Divination seems to be the ability to foresee future events. It is probably more accurate to say that what the various forms of divination actually show us are tendencies and trends. Divination shows you what will most likely happen if you continue on your current course through life. Some of the variables involved are so strong or sizeable that we cannot influence them. Yet many of the variables involved in life can be controlled by the Warrior. Thus outcomes can be altered or modified. We have control over our fate.

This links us back to rebirth, the other symbolism of the Cauldron. Divination allows you to more effectively re-invent yourself. Warriors do not abandon themselves to fate. They use divination to help them chart their course through life. Divination and intuition help the Warrior plan for contingencies.

Any form of divination is simply a tool to help you access the images and impressions forming in your mind. Psychic abilities vary from one person to the next. These tendencies naturally manifest in different ways in different people. The most common form is clair-voyance—visual impressions and images. Other people's psychic talents tend to manifest as clairaudience (auditory impressions), or even clairsentience (simply knowing without any sensory impressions being involved).

There are many traditional forms of divination practiced within the Wiccan community. I have listed some traditional examples of divinatory practices in the Samhain section of the glossary (see page 243). You'll note how these traditional practices do not rely on the psychic abilities of the person using them. They are all more or less "automatic." The people using them are not expected to do anything other than setting them up. This is not the type of divination that I am referring to in this work. What we want to do here is build on the meditation foundation we established in chapter 8. The Warrior needs to take an active role in divination to make it effective.

One very useful and very ancient technique for clairvoyant people is to gaze into a dark bowl full of water. You can use your Chalice for this if you like. As you begin to gaze into the water, shut down all random thoughts as you did in our earlier meditation exercises. Once your mind has become still, open it up and let the impressions come to the surface of your conscious mind.

Record the results in your Book of Shadows. This will help you to identify patterns. It is also important to record the results as people who are adept at divination usually find that while the picture in their mind is very clear at the time of the reading or consultation, it very rapidly fades. Within a half an hour it is difficult to recapture those thoughts. This is because the reader was in an altered state of consciousness that doesn't connect to memory in the same way that normal consciousness does. Recording the results of a reading is therefore very helpful if you intend to refer back to the results at a later date.

This water technique can be applied to many different focus points besides the bowl of water. Some people find that it helps to put a silver coin in the water, representing the power of the moon. The Kahunas of Hawaii take a smooth rock and pour water over it. The Kahuna then gazes into the shiny surface of the rock as it lies in a gourd. Other focus points that may be used for divination include:

◆ Crystals or crystal balls

◆ Mirrors

◆ The palm of your hand

◆ The flames of a fire

If you don't have any of these divination tools handy, you might try closing your eyes and imagining that you are looking into your bowl of water or your skrying glass. This often works as well as using the real thing if you have developed some ability.

Clairaudient people may meditate and listen for voices or sounds. They may meditate on the wind or the sound of waves. Clairsentient people may just close their eyes and let the impressions come. As you can tell from the examples that I have given regarding my own practice of divination, clairsentience is how it works for me. You must experiment with different systems until you identify the ones that work best for you. Once you identify a system that works, you will find that the more you use it, the easier it becomes.

Tarot is the divination system I prefer to use. There are many different available Tarot decks a person can use. The novice reader should seek out one of these decks that appeals or "speaks" to herself. As I mention elsewhere in this book, we all have a personal set of images and symbols that form the language of our subconscious. What Tarot cards do is place images in front of us that help us identify the images in our subconscious. The Tarot deck whose images most closely resemble the symbolic language of your mind is the deck that you will find easiest to use.

I use a slightly different method than the common practice of shuffling and cutting the Tarot cards, and then dealing them off of the top of the deck. If I am reading for others, I commonly let the other person handle the cards first. This helps the person to focus on her concerns, which in turn helps me connect to her. I tell her to hold them, shuffle them, whatever strikes her fancy. I ask that she try to focus on the issue she wants to know about. I warn her that the more precise her query, the more accurate the answer. If you ask a vague question, you'll get a muddled answer. If reading for myself, I hold the cards for a moment and empty my mind of thoughts.

Once the question has been formed, I take the cards and spread them out facedown alongside the area on the table where I will lay out the pattern of cards. I then choose whatever cards seem to call out to me and lay them out. It is as if my hand is operating independently, choosing the cards on its own. I don't hesitate; the principle of daring is extremely important here. Once the cards are laid out, I read them. I record the results in my Book of Shadows. This is important for the beginner; sometimes the meaning may not be clear to you at first and only when the situation fully develops will you understand what you saw in the images on the cards.

As I pointed our earlier, it is especially important to record the results of the reading in your Book of Shadows. Your memory following such meditative states seems to fade rather rapidly. Recording the results immediately following the session is the best way to ensure that you don't lose the results, especially if you intend to refer back to the results at a later date.

In this chapter you have learned some of the symbolism of the Cauldron and the Chalice. You've learned the importance of intuition and divination, and you've experimented with some divination techniques. All that remains in this Book of Water is to learn the meaning of the magick and seasons of this element.

Endnotes

1. Harold Rosenberg. (1960). *The Tradition of the New,* Preface.
2. Henry David Thoreau. (1906). *Journals,* 1850 entry.

14

The Magick and Seasons of Water

There is a harmony
In autumn, and a lustre in its sky,
Which through the summer is not heard or seen,
As if it could not be, as if it had not been!

Percy Bysshe Shelley, "Hymn to Intellectual Beauty"

WATER MAGICK IS the magick of cleansing and purification. You find examples of this in religions such as Santería, which use herbal baths called *despojos*. Despojos are used to dispel evil influences and attract good luck. Steam baths have been used to alter consciousness and raise energy in many cultures. The Native American sweat lodge, the Finnish sauna, and Japanese bathhouse rituals are good examples of this.

The practice of immersing the body in an energetic watery environment or using water to help disperse negative energy and enhance positive energy has been brought into Wicca in a number of ways. One example is the lustral bath; before engaging in ritual activity most Wiccan traditions have the participants take a purifying bath. Another occurs in the Circle-Casting ceremony.

The person casting the Circle charges water mixed with salt and then sprinkles it around the perimeter of the Circle to purify or charge it with their magickal purpose.

In the modern Western world, people have gotten away from baths. The shower is a quicker method of performing your ablutions. They have forgotten that taking the time to relax in the bath is therapeutic. As relaxation of the body permits the chi to flow within you, baths can definitely help improve our flow of chi. In the Book of Earth you learned an important principle of magick: to keep silent. This meditative activity is easiest when you are relaxed. A relaxing bath is a good place to do this. It is like immersing yourself in Bran's magickal Cauldron of rejuvenation. Thus the bath symbolizes the Cauldron, which is the Greater Magickal Weapon of Water.

There are any number of stores that specialize in herbal bath mixtures these days. Bay, bistort, catnip, eyebright, honeysuckle, mugwort, rose, valerian, wormwood, and yarrow are commonly used ingredients. If you are making such a mixture up for yourself, be sure to bind the mixture up in a cheesecloth or a tea ball; you don't want to clog your bath drains with leaves. Edain McCoy's book *Bewitchments* contains some excellent mixtures for use in ritual bathing.

Water isn't just used to purify the body. You should use it to cleanse your ritual implements and Magickal Weapons as well. Immersing such implements in fresh running water is one of the best techniques if you have access to a clean stream (an increasingly difficult-to-find commodity these days). Setting ritual objects overnight in a jar or basin of water can ground out the energy stored within them, thus removing influences that you don't want. If the jar or basin is new, be sure to clean it first to remove any energy that it may have picked up from people who handled it in the warehouse or store. It is traditional to set this purifying basin in the rays of the full moon for best results.

Water is useful for purifying you internally as well. If you aren't getting at least eight glasses of water a day, your body is storing up toxins that it can't dispose of. Remember what I told you about your body being a temple? This is a temple-maintenance program you should engage in.

When discussing grounding in the Book of Earth, I touched on the use of herbal tea. Tea can help relax you, and some teas induce lightly altered states. Some of the more common herbal teas include catnip, cinnamon, dandelion, jasmine, mugwort, peppermint, raspberry, saffron, sage, spearmint, valerian, willow, and wintergreen. An additional benefit of using loose tea leaves is that you can use the pattern of leaves for divination.

In the Book of Earth I discussed various measures you can take to protect yourself. Water in a vase or jar can be used to soak up the negative energy in a room. Adding a little salt or vinegar to the water enhances this effect. If you are concerned about negative energy in your environment, or you are having bad dreams, try this technique. Be sure to empty the jar out periodically and refill it with a fresh solution.

An even better idea is installing a small fountain. The falling water gives off ions that will relax you and enhance the energy of your environment. You will find a similar effect if you cast your Circle near a waterfall or next to a large body of water. One of my favorite early ritual sites was next to a large mountain waterfall that was off to the side of the road on my way home from shift at the police department. Just outside of the room where I write is a small pond with a fountain and waterfall.

Aromatherapy is another form of water magick that is an extension of this. Setting up a small saucer of water over a flame will fill the room with the same ions. Adding a scent appropriate to the magick being performed can enhance the effect.

Seasons of Water

The seasons of Water are the seasons of growth. The late summer and autumn was when the Warrior's campaigning season began to wind down in ancient times. The Warriors returned to their homesteads to help bring in the crops to enable them to survive through the winter. The seasons of water are seasons of harvest, assessment, and review.

Lughnasad is the first harvest festival, occurring on August 1. Lughnasad is the time of year when I begin to harvest the fruits of my labors in the seasons of fire. I add the finishing touches to my writing projects. I promote the books that have been released. I examine the results of my labors. It is a time to take pleasure in accomplishment.

Mabon is our name for the autumnal equinox. Mabon is when I analyze my actions in the past year. This allows me to determine how successful I have been in achieving the objectives and resolutions that I set for myself in my Book of Shadows back in the previous seasons of Earth. This assessment will help me to set my goals for the upcoming cycle of the seasons. It will also help identify problems and mistakes. I can refer to my list of personal characteristics in my Book of Shadows to see if there is something there that I can apply to these problems. With this information, I can develop magickal solutions to these problems. I might also add to this list if I have identified some aspect of my personality that I hadn't considered before. This is a learning process. This knowledge, in turn, will help me become more effective in the next cycle of the year. This review will help me to decide upon the resolutions and objectives that I will commit to at the upcoming Sabbat of Samhain.

In order for me to achieve my magickal objectives I must use my imagination to its fullest. So now it is time to examine the next book—the Book of Fire.

Book Four

THE BOOK OF FIRE

HE ANCIENT ALCHEMISTS recognized the power of transmutation in the element of Fire. The masculine energy of Fire transforms and alters everything it touches without being changed itself. Fire represents virility, potency, and strength. It is the use of fire that separates humans from other animals. Thus, the element of Fire teaches the Wiccan Warrior the lessons of creativity and vision. In the Ritual Circle, the element of Fire is associated to the south. Salamanders are the spirits of Fire. The color of the element of Fire is red, symbolizing fire's smoldering catalytic force.

My imagination is a monastery and I am its monk.

John Keats, in a letter to Percy Shelley

15

Imagination

The man with a new idea is a crank until the idea succeeds.

Mark Twain, "Following the Equator"

As I POINTED out at the beginning of the Book of Water, some people associate the south and the element of Fire with emotions like passion or love. I place all emotions in the realm of the element of Water. I associate the element of Fire with creativity and imagination, since it is a transformative element. Fire changes everything it touches.

What is the imagination? Ralph Waldo Emerson called it "an arm or weapon of the interior energy; only the precursor of the reason."[1] "To Imagine" is to be able to clearly visualize your objective. "Man is an imagining being."[2] This is why one of the sides of the Witch's Pyramid is: *To Imagine.*

Creativity and imagination are aspects of the element of Fire. They are essential elements in the practice of magick. I'm sure that you have noticed by now how many times I have had you do exercises that involved you imagining something. It is all very well to purchase a book on witchcraft or magick and blindly follow the formulas therein. After all, one assumes that all of the stuff in these books works. Why else would the author have put it there?

This is the other side of the Witch's Pyramid that relates to the grail magick of drawing in energy (the other being *To Keep Silent*). It is allowing the inspiration to fill you.

I'm going to resist going off on a tangent here and listing all of the reasons that an author might put ineffective spells in such a book. Suffice to say, one can still find "snake-oil salesmen" in the modern world. Take a close look at some of the "Grimoires" out there and you will quickly grasp what I mean. That does not mean that there aren't a lot of good books of magickal spells out there. Yet even if everything listed in a particular book by reputable authors works for them (they wouldn't have listed it otherwise), it may not work for you for the simple reason that you are a different person.

The trouble with this "cookbook" approach to magick is that it ignores a basic truth—we are all different. What works well for one person may not work as well for another. I have all sorts of things in the Books of Shadows that I copied out of my initiator's Book of Shadows in my early years that didn't work for me. Once you have confirmed that it isn't some mistake or misunderstanding on your part that is interfering with the effectiveness of the magick being performed, you can only conclude that perhaps the technique you are using is basically flawed. This doesn't necessarily mean that every spell you find in someone's else's book of magick is useless. I'm just saying that what works for them might not work for you.

Thus, the twelfth Warrior Precept for your Book of Shadows is:

Twelfth Warrior Precept

Be creative!

Miyamoto Musashi had another way of expressing this precept, "Diligently follow the Path of Two-Swords as one." When I first ask my students what they think Musashi's statement might mean, I get all kinds of interesting answers (many of them quite good, if not exactly what I was seeking). So let me tell you a story about Miyamoto that will help make the meaning of his precept clear.

In the sixteenth century, when Miyamoto lived, the Samurai carried a pair of swords called the Katana. One sword was long and one short. When faced with an aggressive opponent, the Samurai carefully considered the situation and his environment, and chose one of the two swords. The chosen sword was grasped with two hands. This is the way that everyone was taught—two hands, one sword.

Miyamoto taught himself how to use the Katana. When faced with an opponent, he drew both of his swords, holding one in each hand. The way Miyamoto saw it was this—two hands, two swords. This caused considerable consternation. Opponents would complain that this was not traditional, or that it was improper, or that it was unfair. Nontraditional it may have been, but it was extremely effective. Miyamoto was never defeated.

Can you see the meaning of the precept now? Don't do something because "this is the way that it has always been done." Don't do things simply because they are "traditional." Use a particular technique because it *works*. French moralist Marquis de Luc Vauvenargues once said:

> Most people grow old within a small circle of ideas, which they have not discovered for themselves. There are perhaps less wrong-minded people than thoughtless.[3]

This is the sort of attitude you will find in remote rural villages where things are done a certain way only because that's the way they've always been done. Being out of touch with new developments sometimes leads to stagnant thinking. People in isolated societies often fall into an existence defined by routines. Yet there is always something new to learn.

In the Book of Earth I touched briefly upon the subject of eliminating habits and routine. I pointed out how routines and habits can set you up to be ambushed. A Warrior has no routines. This is just another example of that principle. The Warrior must be spontaneous and fluid rather than a creature of habit.

This does not mean that routines and regimens don't have their place. But the Wiccan Warrior is not fettered by them; they shouldn't prevent flexibility and innovation. They shouldn't be a liability. If a change is called for, the Wiccan Warrior doesn't hesitate to change. Bruce Lee put it this way, "Set patterns, incapable of adaptability, of pliability, only offer a better cage. Truth is outside of all patterns."[4]

A Wiccan becomes a Warrior by seeking results, leading us to the thirteenth Warrior Precept:

Thirteenth Warrior Precept

Do not engage in useless activity.

This doesn't mean to say that you shouldn't go looking in books or seek out new instructors and try new things out. There is nothing wrong with experimentation. That is how you will find out what works for you. What it does mean is that if you find that a particular technique or "spell" doesn't work, you should set it aside. Perhaps it won't work for you at your present stage of development. Maybe it isn't a technique that will work for you at all. If this is the case, toss it out.

That is why you use a Book of Shadows as a working journal. This is where you will record results. You should record the failures too. You should periodically review old entries; sometimes something that you've recently learned will give you the key to something that didn't work for you before.

Let's look at ways of using your imagination to achieve your magickal goals. There is an old adage in magick, "Be careful what you ask for! You'll probably get it!" If you haven't carefully considered exactly what you want or haven't been able to accurately visualize your goal, then what you ask for will probably not meet your expectations or requirements. So an accurate and creative imagination is essential to magick.

Visualization

In the Book of Earth we looked at meditation exercises designed to improve your concentration. Now let's modify these to help you focus on your magickal goal. In the previous meditation exercises you had your eyes open. Once you have mastered the ability to focus on this object for ten minutes or more without stray thoughts entering into your head, try this variation. Close your eyes and imagine an object like a candle flame or a feather suspended in front of you. Rather than using an actual object to focus on, simply imagine the candle flame flickering or the feather moving as you breathe in and out.

It is just a short step from this exercise to closing your eyes and imagining your magical purpose. The more vivid this image is, the more effective the magick. Dr. Jonn Mumford, a Western doctor trained in Eastern medicine and yoga, teaches that to visualize something fully you have to build a *C-A-S-E:*

- The *C* stands for *Color.* Visualize an object in the most vivid colors you can imagine.

- The *A* stands for *Action.* Moving objects are always easier to focus on, just ask anybody who creates TV commercials. If you are visualizing an automobile, put it in motion, make the wheels spin.

- The *S* stands for *Size.* In Western culture we imagine things as being rather small because we have been taught that one's consciousness resides in the brain. It's as if we have to make the object small to fit inside our head. Instead, make the object that you are visualizing *huge*.

◆ The *E* stands for *Emotion*. Recent studies into ESP and related phenomena have proven the old belief that such abilities (and magick) work best when the person(s) doing it are very emotionally involved in the process.[5]

Be careful how you do this. For example, when doing healing magick, one should always work with positive images rather than negative ones, to keep the focus clear. For example, if I said to you, "Do not think of a cat," your subconscious would conjure up an image of a cat so that you could see what it is I *don't* want you to see. Therefore thoughts like "be healthy" and "long life" would work better than "no more illness."

Try imagining different objects using this system. Imagine the object in vivid (even nonsensical) colors. Make the object move— have it rotate or flip over. Imagine each object several times its normal size. Put as much emotion into these exercises as you can. Keep a record of your visualization work in your Book of Shadows.

When you can hold one of these images in your mind for a few minutes with your eyes closed, try this variation. Rub your hands together to warm them up. Cup your palms over your eyes and stare into the darkness thus created without closing them. Imagine the same objects floating before you in this darkness. Once you have been able to master this, try doing it with your eyes uncovered and open. Make the object so real that you feel that you can touch it. Put it on the table or grass in front of you.

Another useful exercise is to close your eyes and imagine the room or outdoor setting in which you placed yourself to meditate. Imagine what the room or yard around you looked like before you closed your eyes. Take a mental tour of the room or yard and examine the objects in it, one by one. Once you feel that you have examined each object thoroughly, open your eyes to check the object. See how close you were in your visualization. Once you have mastered this, close your eyes and imagine you are getting up and walking into another room or into another part of the yard. Examine everything around you. Eventually you can progress to the point where you are leaving your house or yard and moving around your neighborhood. Keep track of how far you have been able to go in your Book of Shadows.

The Astral Temple

When I spoke of sacred space in chapter 5, I pointed out that the Circle had an astral or psychic equivalent that I will call the astral temple. This is the sacred space you create entirely within your own mind. This is a place where you can go to connect with aspects of the divine, or simply to recharge yourself. It may be your private place, or you may share it with others in your Coven. It can be as simple of elaborate as you wish. You can modify it at will.

To set up your astral temple you must first decide what kind of temple you want. This is quite easy if you are solitary; you only have to please yourself. If you are part of a Coven that wishes to set up an astral temple, you will all need to arrive at a consensus as to what you want to set up. People often imagine their temple as having the architecture of the culture that appeals to them. Use whatever you are comfortable with; you may imagine it to be an Egyptian colonnade, a Greek acropolis, or a Circle of standing stones. Groups might decide that certain portions or rooms in their temple may be set aside for individual members to "customize" in any way that suits them.

You go to your astral temple in meditation. One way to do this is a variation of the previous exercise where you close your eyes and take an imaginary journey around your property. In this case, you close your eyes and take a voyage inward. Roughly in the middle of your skull is the pineal gland. We will use this as a focal point to start this exercise.

Once you have closed your eyes, imagine you are in a dark room. Imagine yourself turning around and inward to face the pineal gland. Imagine it as a crystal glowing brightly in the dark and mounted on a door. Go to that door and open it. Through it you pass into the sacred space where your astral temple is situated. If this is your first trip here, you will have to build this temple up into the structure you desire. For example, if you want this space to be a Circle of standing stones, you would imagine yourself emerging from the doorway into a field or grove. Here you would set up the stones in any pattern or configuration that you desire. Don't worry about the doorway through which you entered this astral space. You only have to think of it and it will reappear for you. You can incorporate it into the structure you are creating if you wish.

In this process, visualization is crucial. Don't restrict this to your sense of sight. Involve all of your senses. You should not only see an image of your temple, you should hear the sounds there, feel the wind on your face and in your hair, and smell the scents in your astral temple.

Why create such an astral temple? One reason is that it serves as a link between your conscious mind and subconscious. I often go to my astral temple to encounter aspects of deity; I find them there waiting for me. Sometimes I find tokens or symbols they have left for me to find. One might find messages from other Wiccans. These will help you to identify the things in your life that you need to work on. What occurs in this astral temple resonates through your world and can manifest in it.

Once you have done in your astral temple what you went there to accomplish, simply return to the doorway and imagine yourself walking through it. Turn to close this door, facing that glowing crystal. Take a deep breath and turn outward. When you are ready, open your eyes.

Some people find it easier to imagine a staircase descending into the astral realm than a simple doorway. Try this and see how it works for you. If you are a city dweller, it may be easier for you to imagine an elevator or a subway train that lets you off at your astral temple. It doesn't matter how you imagine getting there, it is getting there that counts.

Another useful technique for accessing the astral temple is to close your eyes and imagine you are standing in moonlight in front of a body of dark water. Imagine cold mist rising from the water. This is astral mist. Imagine the mist enveloping you. The mist transforms your surroundings, and when it dissipates, you find yourself in your psychic temple. This is the sort of image that Marion Zimmer Bradley invoked in *The Mists of Avalon*. To get to the Blessed Isle, you had to journey on a barge through the magickal mists. To come back you simply imagine the mists enveloping you again and returning you to the mundane world.

A more advanced way to enter your astral temple is to use a mirror as a portal. For this your eyes remain open, as you are meditating in front of a mirror. Many people find it easier to see psychically in a mirror. In it they can build their astral images and the crystal structure of the mirror is said to hold the energy.

For this mirror exercise, your eyes will stay open. At first, it is probably best to do this in a darkened room with the only light being a small one directed at you. This way, the only thing you will see in the mirror before you is your image. Around it you can build up the astral temple. Once it is constructed, you simply step into it in your imagination in a similar fashion to the "doorway" you used in the previous exercise.

You won't know which system works best for you until you try them out yourself. Experiment and see what works best for your situation. As with dreaming, it is a good idea to have your journal or Book of Shadows handy so you can record any impressions or messages you received before they start to fade. You were in a different state of consciousness, and memory does not work there the same way as it does in waking consciousness.

If you're making this inward journey as a group exercise, one person should direct the astral journey of the rest of the group. This works because, even in a deep trance, a person can still hear the facilitator, even if it isn't on a conscious level. Leading a guided meditation or trance is pretty straightforward, and if you are part of a group, it is quite easy to accomplish. Here are some tips for the facilitator to keep in mind:

◆ The facilitator should speak in time with the breathing of the person you are directing, preferably on the exhalation of his breath. If you are doing this for a group, this becomes more difficult. You will have to allow enough time for the breathing of the participants to synchronize.

◆ The facilitator should always have the participants turn inward from reality and then onward to whatever vision is to be experienced. The mirror working technique doesn't work that well for more than two people.

◆ The facilitator should try not to use negatives. In other words, avoid saying things like "don't." Rather than telling the subject what not to do, give positive directions. Tell them what they *can* do.

◆ The facilitator should never give a command when leading a trance. Use the words "may," "could," "if," or "might." Some people will naturally put up resistance to imperative words like "must" or "shall" and this may interfere with their concentration. If you notice that a person is resisting, work with it rather than against it.

◆ Visualization is crucial. Don't restrict this to the sense of sight. Involve all of the senses. Get the participants to see where they are, to hear the sounds there, to feel and smell the place being imagined.

◆ Be careful of the depth you take your subjects to. This can be a problem if you want them to make verbal responses. If you take them too deep, they may not be able to respond, and they may not be able to remember. If you discover that your subject is in too deep a trance to respond, ask for finger signals. It is possible to have them come up to a higher level by having them visualize themselves ascending stairs or floating up to a higher level.

◆ Be alert to physical cues in your subjects. Watch their breathing, eye movements, and skin color. These will give you an indication of what the subject is experiencing, and whether they are feeling fear or discomfort.

◆ If the subject is in distress, *don't panic! Don't* lose your cool, and try to bring them out quickly. If your subject is in distress, having encountered an alarming vision or entity in their vision, give them a tool to deal with it. Tell them that they have a Magickal Weapon or abilities to take care of the problem.

◆ It often helps your subjects if you tell them that they will have a "clear and vivid recollection" of their experience.

The astral temple can also be used as a meeting place for several people who aren't able to meet physically. At a pre-arranged time you and several others can meditate wherever you happen to find yourself and meet with the others in your astral temple. This is a form of astral projection.

In this chapter you have discovered the fourth side of the Witch's Pyramid: *To Imagine.* You've added another two Warrior Precepts to your Book of Shadows: (1) *Be creative,* and (2) *Do not engage in useless activity.* You've learned visualization exercises that will enhance your magickal ability. Next we will learn how to use the Weapons of Fire to focus our energy.

Endnotes

1. Ralph Waldo Emerson. (1870). *Society and Solitude,* "Books."

2. Gaston Bachelard. (1960). *The Poetics of Reverie,* ch. 2, sct. 10.

3. Marquis de Luc Vauvenargues. (1746). *Refléxions et Maximes,* no. 236.

4. Bruce Lee. (1975). *Tao of Jeet Kune Do,* p. 15.

5. Dr. Jonn Mumford. From the *Creative Visualization* audiotape. Date unknown.

16

The Wand and the Spear

What ever you can do or dream you can do, begin it . . .
boldness has power, magic and genius in it.

Goethe

IN SOME TRADITIONS, the Wand or Staff are associated with the element of Air, while the Sword and the Athame are assigned to the element of Fire. The reasoning usually advanced to support this is that fire is used to shape and temper the metal blade. I have even heard people argue that the shape of the double-edged blade resembles a flame. Yet it is wood that produces the flame that tempers the metal. Thus I classify the Wand and the Staff or Spear as Weapons of Fire.

Weapons of Fire should be made by the person who intends to use them. Traditionally the Lesser Weapon of Fire, the Wand, is made of willow, elder, oak, apple, peach, hazel, or cherrywood. I have two, one willow and one birch. Many Wiccan traditions hold that the length of the Wand should be the distance from the tips of the fingers to the elbow (one cubit). Wands may be quite plain, painted, or inscribed with symbols. Some people will insert a piece of metal, or have an iron rod running inside the Wand's length to improve its conductive qualities, but I consider this unnecessary.

The Greater Weapon of Fire is the Spear or Staff. This is traditionally made of woods like birch, willow, or hazel, which form long, straight branches. The traditional Stang is a Staff with a fork at the top, which resembles the horns or antlers of the male animal. Like the Wand, the Staff may be plain or decorated. My Stang is a forked birch branch with a spiral pattern of leaves carved around the shaft.

The Spear is one of the earliest weapons known to man. It was originally just a sharpened stick. The Sumerians employed massed ranks of spearmen in their army as early as 3,000 B.C.E. A variation is the arrow, which was used as a military weapon from Egyptian times to the Middle Ages in Europe and even longer in the East. These projectile weapons were an early form of "artillery." Bowmen and spear throwers were able to project their spears and arrows great distances. Eventually the invention of cannons brought the element of Fire fully into the picture.

The magick Wand is one of the most common symbols of magick in popular Western culture. The Wand is a phallic symbol; like the phallus, it projects life energy. The idea that the magick actually comes out of the magick Wand (a Lesser Weapon) is what gives laypeople the impression that magick requires magick Wands.

I would rather you thought of the Wand, Spear, and Staff as focussing tools or as projectors of energy than sources of magickal power. The Weapons of Fire are Magickal Tools you can focus through. They act as a conduit or a channel through which you can connect to the universe around you. Remember in chapter 6 my point about teaching yourself to receive or project energy with either hand? A similar principle applies in this situation. You should learn to use wield the Weapons of Fire with either hand, or two-handed. The Wand or Staff are focussing tools; you can use them to focus the chi both inward and outward.

Some forms of magick require the Warrior to send energy long distances. The Weapons of Fire can be used to focus your energy to facilitate this. This is one of the lessons of the element of Fire. In chapter 5 we experimented with a technique called "Holding the Ball." Let me show you now how to adapt this technique to allow you to project energy out from you.

Start once again from the Entering Tranquility posture, raising your arms in front of you to hold an energetic "ball" against your chest. Spread your fingers and don't let your hands touch. As you inhale, it expands and glows; imagine the ball of energy pressing out against your arms and chest. As you exhale, it contracts and spins forward. Let this ball of energy grow for a while. When you feel ready, draw your hands back toward your shoulders as if putting your hands behind this ball to push it away from you. Then, with a pushing motion, extend your arms out straight in front of you. Hold them out for a moment and feel the energy streaming through your body and out of your hands at your magickal objective. In your mind's eye, see the energy as a blue light shining out of your palms toward your objective.

A variation of this technique is known in Chi Kung as "Pushing Mountains." Starting in the Entering Tranquility posture, place your palms, fingers pointing upward, at chest level at the sides of your body, with your elbows pointing back. Gently push out both hands as if pushing something away from you. Breathe out and visualize the chi flowing out of the palms of your hands toward your objective. Inhale and bring your hands back to the starting position. Repeat this procedure several times. To an observer, this looks a bit like mimicking pushups while standing up. You should feel as if the energy flowing out of you is powerful enough to push a mountain away from you.

Now let's look at how the Wand or Spear can be used as a tool to help focus this energy stream. There are a number of ways to use the Wand to send out magickal energy. I have found that one of the most effective is a variation of a Chi Kung exercise called

"Lifting the Sky." To do this, start in Entering Tranquility posture, arms at your sides, holding the Wand in one hand. Bring your hands together in front of you, grasping the Wand with both hands. Keep your arms and elbows straight. Move your arms forward and then upward in a continuous arc. As you do this, breathe in. Follow the Wand with your eyes. Imagine the cosmic energy flowing into you. As your arms point straight up, you will find yourself looking up. Pause a moment, holding your breath. Then push the Wand up slightly as if poking the ceiling or the sky. Imagine the energy flowing through you and out of the end of the Wand toward your magickal objective. Once you have done this, separate your hands, taking the Wand in one hand. Lower your arms to your sides in a continuous arc while exhaling. Stand in Entering Tranquility posture for a moment to let your energy come back into balance.

It isn't necessary to have the Wand pointing directly at what you are directing your chi toward. Imagine this to be a sort of "magickal artillery." You are directing the energy toward the target in an arc, like the arc of a shell from a howitzer. If it helps you to imagine a line-of-sight projection, point your Wand out toward your objective instead of straight up in the air.

If you have trouble visualizing the flow of energy through your Wand, try this: Take the Wand in your hand and point it in the direction you want the energy to go. Squeeze the Wand in your hand as hard as you can. Feel the muscles in your arm tighten between your hand and shoulder. Now slowly relax, starting at the shoulder and working down to your hand. Imagine the energy starting to flow down your arm as the tension in it dissolves. As this wave of energy reaches your hand it will stream through the Wand.

You may experience a number of sensations when you are successfully sending energy through the Wand. Some people perceive a distortion like heat waves in the air around the Wand.

Some people perceive waves of color on or around the Wand, or a beam of light streaming out of it. Others may sense that the Wand is vibrating or humming. Remember how I pointed out earlier that different people experience psychic phenomena in different ways? Everyone is different, so you must find out for yourself how you perceive this flow of chi.

Sending energy toward a magickal objective isn't the only reason to send energy through a Weapon of Fire. As I pointed out earlier in the section on grounding, the Greater Weapons of Fire can be used as "lightning rods" to ground out surplus energy. The Staff, Stang, or Spear is preferred for this purpose as you can do it standing or sitting. You simply hold the Staff upright on the ground in front of you with both hands and let the surplus energy flow into the ground through the Staff. You can use a Wand to do this too, but you'll have to squat down to do it, so the Greater Weapons are more comfortable for this technique.

Now earlier in this Book of Fire I mentioned that the side of the Witch's Pyramid that we were dealing with was *To Imagine*. I went on to point out that this is one of those "grail processes" in which you let the inspiration fill you. Yet for the last few paragraphs I've been describing many ways of using the Weapons of Fire to send energy out of you. Once again, there is no contradiction here. Weapons of Fire can also be used to draw energy into oneself. All you have to do is control the flow with your intent. Try the "Lifting the Sky" exercise, drawing "sky" energy in instead of sending chi out. This is a good exercise for promoting overall energy flow. You might also try reversing the lightning-rod technique, drawing energy up out of the earth, and into your body through your arms. Record the results in your Book of Shadows.

Once again, try not try rely solely on your personal reserves of energy when you do magickal work. I know I made this point earlier, but I see so many beginners making this mistake that it is worth emphasizing it to drive the point home. In magick, you must make yourself the channel through which the energy of the universe flows.

Sending Shared Energy

In the Book of Spirit I asked you to experiment with ways of sharing energy within the Circle. Let's look at some ways that shared energy can be sent out of the circle to a distant magickal objective.

One way to share energy is for one person in charge of the ritual to direct or use the energy sent to them by one or more others. In this technique only one person's will is focussed on the objective—that of the person in charge. The others are simply sending their energy to this person. This is a common practice when the person in charge is "channeling" or "aspecting." The advantage is that only one person, the one sending the energy, has to visualize the objective. The only weakness is that if the person directing the energy is not so good at channeling the chi through themselves, some of the energy will be lost in the process.

Another way to share energy is for each of the participants to raise energy and send it individually to a common objective. The participants raise energy as a group, but each uses his or her own will to direct it. Toning can be used in this situation as well. The drawback here is that each individual is only as effective as their ability to visualize the common objective. However, this technique avoids the "weakest link" problem of sending it through one person.

Either way, the best way of visualizing this process of projecting energy out of the Magick Circle is a technique that Wiccans call the Cone of Power. Picture the Magick Circle as the base, with you standing at its center. You are building up a swirling cloud of energy in the Circle that you then project outward. The objective that this energy is to be directed to becomes the apex of the Cone of Power you are sending out.

Dance is another group exercise for raising energy for a Cone of Power. Yet dance may not seem like a Warrior activity to the uninitiated. A fellow Wiccan Warrior, Paul Tuitean, once told me that the difference between a soldier and a Warrior was that "soldiers march, Warriors dance." This isn't just a metaphor. Dance is another of the ancient ways of raising energy and working off stress. Anyone who has ever been in a dojo watching someone performing Karate *katas* (or "forms"), or watched people in a park going through the flowing motions of the Yang Short form of Tai Chi, certainly cannot doubt that this is a form of dance.

Chanting or singing while dancing in a Circle has become one of the more popular ways of raising energy in Wiccan Circles. The songs used are brief, repetitive rhyming verses, a form of *dharani*. A dharani is a single-phrase mantra (we'll discuss mantras in chapter 21). There are many such songs to choose from. One of the most popular is simply an invocation to the many aspects of the Goddess, "Isis, Astarte, Diana, Hecate, Demeter, Kali, Innana."[1] Chants are often combined with dance. The dance should be relaxed and flowing. "The ultimate aim of dancing is to be able to move without thinking, to *be* danced."[2] I'll go into the subject of chanting in more detail later in the Book of Air.

Dancing often includes the use of mudras or gestures. The Tantric term *mudra* (pronounced "moodra") is from a Sanskrit root meaning "to seal or close-off." A mudra is a gesture. Traditional Wiccan ritual is full of mudras. If you've seen someone tracing the pentagram in the air with their fingers or Athame while calling the quarters of a Circle, you've seen a mudra. Mudras of this sort can be used at the completion of a dance to seal the magick worked, and ground surplus energy before going on to other things. You may recall that earlier I had you clench your fists to seal off the subchakras there in one of the grounding and centering exercises. This is a sealing mudra.

One way of raising energy through dance is to have the participants join hands and do a circular dance while chanting a particular mantra. As the energy increases, they go faster and chant louder. When the energy has peaked in the Circle, the priestess or priest leading the dance will signal the participants by slowing to a halt and letting go of the hands of those on either side. The participants quickly turn inward and direct the energy thus raised to wherever it is to be sent. The Maypole dance is a perfect example of this; the central pole is just a larger version of the Staff and serves as a focal point.

A popular variation is the spiral dance, in which the leader of the dance leads the Coven in a spiral inward. When the leader reaches the middle, he or she reverses direction, leading the group spiraling back out again. Thus, the group briefly has a double line of dancers passing in opposite directions. Once the energy peaks, the leader reforms the Circle and stops the dance, allowing the dancers to release the energy raised as in the previous example.

While both of these examples involve group practices, the solitary Warrior does not need anyone but himself to dance ecstatically to raise energy. Once the energy peaks, stop and raise your arms toward your magickal objective. Imagine the Cone of Power forming with the objective at its apex. Let the energy stream out of your palms with your fingers spread apart.

In this chapter you have learned the symbolism of the Wand and Spear. You've learned how to use the Weapons of Fire to focus magickal energy. You've added more techniques for sharing energy to your Book of Shadows. I've discussed the Cone of Power. All that remains in this Book of Fire is to examine the importance of the seasons and magick of this element.

Endnotes

1. A chant written by Deena Metzger.
2. John Blacking. (1973). *How Musical Is Man?*

17

The Magick and Seasons of Fire

Summer set lip to earth's bosom bare
And left the flushed print in a poppy there.

Francis Thompson, "The Poppy"

FIRE IS AN element of transformation. For centuries humankind has used it to transform and shape things. Like the element of Water, you can also use it to purge unwanted influences from your life.

Fire Magick

Fire magick is a very effective way to help you break away from habits or relationships obstructing your progress or adversely affecting your well-being.

Here is an example. Take a piece of paper and write down the things obstructing you. Your entries may include negative emotions, fears, habits, obsessions, or unfavorable relationships. Imagine that these things are in your past as you write them down.

Next, burn the paper. You can use a candle to set it alight and leave it to burn on the ground, on the hearth, or in a Cauldron. You can toss it on to the Sabbat bonfire. Visualize these negative ties dissolving as the paper burns. Visualize your life free of these limitations from this point on. Affirm to yourself as you do this that such elements of your past are no longer a part of you. Scream or shout it out if this helps you put the necessary emotional charge into it.

An effective variation is to wrap the paper around a small quantity of some flammable powder such as flour or sugar before tossing it into the flames. The resulting flash when you toss it into the bonfire is a very satisfying visual image that may assist you in visualizing the end result. The group I have celebrated Beltaine with for the past several years has handed out readymade paper bundles like this to celebrants. You just put whatever you want to leave behind into this bundle and then heave it into the fire.

Candle Magick

This is a very old magickal technique, and is a variation of the meditation exercises I described earlier. In a way, the candle is a sort of Wand; like a wooden torch, it holds a flame. The candle serves as a tool that helps the Warrior to focus his energy. The color of the candle may be chosen to represent the type of work to be done. This helps the Warrior to visualize the purpose of the magick. Use the table of color attributes in chapter 11 to select the color of the candle you will use in your magickal work.

Having chosen the appropriate colored candle to represent the purpose of the magick being done, you must focus the object of your desire on the candle. Anointing the candle with oil while thinking of the objective is one way of helping to focus this intent. Writing words associated to the magickal objective on the candle is another way for the Warrior to focus his intent and enhance the magickal energy.

Once the candle is prepared, take a moment to focus your mind on the object of your magick. As you light the candle, imagine the chain of events that will occur and see the successful completion of your magick. You may meditate on the purpose of the magick while gazing at the candle once it is lit, if you wish. This will certainly intensify the result. However, unless you've used a very small candle, watching the candle burn itself out can take a long time. The beauty of this system is that the candle can be left burning in some safe location where it does not present a fire hazard. You can then leave it to do its work. It doesn't matter that the candle may not be visible to you. The fact that it is there will be in the back of your mind. Every time you think of the candle, it refocuses your will on the objective. This is the same principle involved in the use of votive candles at shrines. It helps to bring the mind back to the memories involved.

Watch the candle carefully for a few minutes before you leave it to do its work. Note any unusual effects or impressions in your Book of Shadows. These notes will help you to identify patterns; many people note certain effects in the flame when they do successful candle magick. These effects may vary from person to person, just as they do in the use of the Wand or Athame. Identifying such effects will help you to gauge the effectiveness of your magick. If you don't perceive the effects, this may be an indication you have made and error somewhere in the process.

If you want to put more energy into a magickal project, you may want to light one candle each day over a period of several days. If this is your intent, it is best to do your candle magick at the same time each day.

Seasons of Fire

The Season of Fire is the season of summer. The summer season was the campaigning season for Warriors in ancient times. This is when the weather was most favorable to campaigns and action. The action planned in the seasons of earth and commenced in the Seasons of Air is well underway. The seasons of Fire are seasons of action and achievement.

Beltaine, April 30, is halfway through the cycle of seasons. It is a fertility festival. This is the time of year when my projects are well underway. It is a time of action and exploiting opportunities. I am fully committed to my chosen courses of action. I am putting maximum effort into realizing my goals. I am doing magick to enhance this process. As Beltaine is a celebration of fertility, it is an excellent opportunity to put magickal energy into whatever projects you have on the go. You refer to your Book of Shadows to find techniques you can use to maximize results.

Litha is our name for the autumnal equinox. Litha is when I monitor my progress to see if there is anything else that I can do to help my plans come into fruition. It is a time to make adjustments.

The last thing that I need to make my magickal objectives come true is the will to succeed. Thus it is time to examine the last book, the Book of Air.

Book Five

THE BOOK OF AIR

HE ELEMENT OF Air represents the power of the mind, which, like the wind, is invisible yet powerful. The masculine energy of Air is the power of thought used to conceptualize and shape the world around you. For the Wiccan Warrior, the principal lesson of Air is the power of will. In the Wiccan Circle, the element of Air is associated with the east. Thus it represents the power of beginnings. Sylphs are the spirits of Air. The color of the element of Air is yellow, which represents the lights of the heavens.

My imagination makes me human and makes me a fool; it gives me all the world and exiles me from it.

Ursula K. Le Guin,
"Winged: the Creatures on my Mind"

18

Will

Excellence, then, is not an act, but a habit.

Aristotle

AIR IS THE element of the eastern quarter of the Wiccan's Circle. The element of Air is associated with will and mental disciplines. Earlier in this work we spoke of how to raise and focus energy. In this Book of Air, we will talk about how to direct this energy to its objective. Without will, the magickal energy you release will be diffuse and ineffective. Therefore the Book of Air must begin with a discussion of the last side of the Witch's Pyramid: *To Will*.

There is an old Zen adage, *munen muso*, which means, "where there is no intention, there is no thought of moving." In order to use magickal energy, the Wiccan must use his will. As I pointed out above, in Eastern philosophies this magickal energy is known as chi. So another way of stating this is to say that chi (energy) follows your intent or will.

To Will is the other side of the Witch's Pyramid concerned with sending out energy (the other side being *To Dare*). Remember I said that daring was the magickal "pressure" that helped to send

the energy out of you? Daring is the switch that turns the magickal energy on, to send it on its way. Will is the steering mecha-
nism that directs the energy to the objective. Without will, the
energy that you sent out wouldn't go anywhere. It would simply
disperse randomly into the universe.

To will is to have an unwavering purpose. Will is the channeling of your awareness to focus precisely on that which you want
with burning intensity. If you don't know where you're going,
then you'll probably arrive someplace else. To develop your will is
to teach yourself to clearly define your objective. Concentration is
essential to magick. If you simply broadcast the energy that you
raise in no particular direction, or with a very vague or general
focus, it will not have much effect. But if all of your energy is
focused on a very narrow purpose, or on a very clearly defined
goal, it will invariably succeed. This is the same principle that
makes a punch so effective in Karate; energy (chi) is concentrated
and focused with intent.

One recent explanation presented to explain magick and psy-
chokinetic phenomena involves a principle in quantum physics
called Schrödinger's Wave Equation or "Wave Function." The
equation predicts the probability that the measurable attributes
of a particle will have a certain value. For example, one can com-
pute the probability that a molecule of water will escape through
the walls of a sealed glass jar and be found outside of it. This
means that because all matter has the properties of quantum
duality, there is a calculable probability that if I took a flight, leaving my wife Phoenix behind in Vancouver, I might bump into her
on the streets of Chicago. Until the event happens (in other
words, when the observation is made) only the probabilities exist.
When the measurement is made, then the values of the attribute
are certain and the equation with its probabilities is said to "collapse" to an actual event with a probability equal to "1."

The implication for magick is this. From this viewpoint, one could say that practicing magick is the process of causing Schrödinger's Wave Equation to collapse in the place required to achieve the desired result. The key to this process is will. Will provides the intent that causes the collapse in the correct place. I encourage the reader to explore this subject of quantum physics, psychokinesis, and "intentionality" in more detail in former astronaut Edgar Mitchell's recent book, *The Way of the Explorer.*

So you can see that, in magick, maintaining your focus is essential. Don't let yourself be diverted or distracted from your purpose. "Don't exchange what you want most for what you want at the moment."[1] If your purpose or attention wavers, the energy is dispersed and the outcome of your magickal work will be less effective.

To will is to have strong self-discipline. Self-discipline is the hallmark of the Warrior.[2] This is not merely a physical discipline such as one finds in the martial arts or in athletic competition. It also involves the training of the mind, which is one of the Lesser Magickal Weapons. Self-discipline is the skill that allows you to persistently pursue your goals.

The Warrior is goal-oriented. He does not let anything divert him from his purpose. Remember what we were told by the Charge of the Goddess, "Keep pure your highest ideal; strive ever towards it, let naught stop you or turn you aside." Persistence is one of the most effective tools that you have. I have known many people to overcome any number of faults or handicaps with sheer persistence.

Oliver Wendell Holmes once told us that "what's important is not necessarily where you are, but in what direction you are going." In order to create the reality that you want, you need to establish some precise objectives. Start a new page in your Book of Shadows and start a list of your objectives. This is a true "wish list." Don't hold back. "Goals are dreams with deadlines."[3]

You can break this down into weekly, monthly, or yearly objectives. As I pointed out in the Book of Earth, every Samhain, at the beginning of the Wiccan year, I review my objectives of the following year and formulate new ones. For example, I determine the minimum number of books and articles I intend to produce in the coming twelve months. At each Sabbat I review and renew my list of lesser objectives. For example, I might decide at Yule that by Imbolc I will have mastered a particular technique of Tai Chi. I set weekly objectives for myself, too. For example, I review my investigative files at the beginning of each week to allocate time to each of the pending investigations.

Try to avoid taking on more than you can handle. This used to be a big problem for me. I would quickly agree to people's requests without taking time to think of how I was going to fit it in with all of the other commitments I had already made. Before I knew it I was snowed under and unable to honor a lot of the commitments I had made. You have to review every aspect of your life and prioritize. Follow the advice of General Colin Powell, "Don't eye the top of the ladder, eye the next rung."

The following story illustrates this point very well.

Big Rocks

One day an expert in time management was speaking to a group of business students and, to drive home a point, used an illustration those students will never forget. As he stood in front of the group of high powered overachievers he said, "Okay, time for a quiz."

Then he pulled out a one-gallon, wide-mouthed Mason jar and set it on the table in front of him. Then he produced about a dozen fist-sized rocks and carefully placed them, one at a time, into the jar. When the jar was filled to the top and no more rocks would fit inside, he asked, "Is this jar full?"

Everyone in the class said, "Yes."

Then he said, "Really?" He reached under the table and pulled out a bucket of gravel. Then he dumped some gravel in and shook the jar causing pieces of gravel to work themselves down into the space between the big rocks. Then he asked the group once more, "Is the jar full?"

By this time the class was on to him. "Probably not," one of them answered.

"Good!" he replied. He reached under the table and brought out a bucket of sand. He started dumping the sand in the jar and it went into all of the spaces left between the rocks and the gravel. Once more he asked the question, "Is this jar full?"

"No!" the class shouted. Once again he said, "Good."

Then he grabbed a pitcher of water and began to pour it in until the jar was filled to the brim. Then he looked at the class and asked, "What is the point of this illustration?"

One eager beaver raised his hand and said, "The point is, no matter how full your schedule is, if you try really hard you can always fit some more things in it!"

"No," the speaker replied, "that's not the point. The truth this illustration teaches us is: If you don't put the big rocks in first, you'll never get them in at all." What are the "big rocks" in your life?

God; your children; your loved ones; your education; your dreams; a worthy cause; teaching or mentoring others; doing things that you love; time for yourself; your health; your significant other. Remember to put these Big Rocks in first or you'll never get them in at all. If you sweat the little stuff (the gravel, the sand, the water) then you'll fill your life with little things you worry about that don't really matter, and you'll never have the real quality time you need to spend on the big, important stuff (the big rocks).

So, tonight, or in the morning, when you are reflecting on this short story, ask yourself this question: What are the "big rocks" in my life?[4]

Decisiveness is essential for the Wiccan Warrior. You won't ever accomplish anything if you can't make a decision about what course of action to take. This does not mean to say that you should rush into a situation. Careful consideration and planning are often the keys to success. This is the lesson of the Fifth Warrior Precept: *Do not be negligent, even in trifling matters.*

General George Patton once said that an average plan quickly and boldly executed was often better than a superior plan that had been planned at length. What is often more important is not what decision to make but rather that you take decisive action quickly. I have found over and over again in my police work that there is usually more than one way to accomplish something. Yet nothing gets accomplished if you don't make a decision to act. Sun Tzu had made a similar comment centuries earlier, "The quality of decision is like the well-timed swoop of a falcon which enables it to strike and destroy its victim."[5]

Having made your decision about what you hope to accomplish in your magick, you will have to focus your energy on this goal to achieve it. I've already shown you some focussing techniques; later in this Book of Air I will show you some more involving the Weapons of Air.

In this chapter you have discovered the last side of the Witch's Pyramid: *To Will.* We have examined the importance of focus and self-discipline. You've listed objectives and set priorities. You've learned the importance of decisiveness. In the next chapter you will discover the mysteries of initiation.

Endnotes

1. Lynn Greenling. *Weight Watchers' Leader.*
2. Robert Moore and Douglas Gillette. (1992). *The Warrior Within: Accessing the Knight in the Male Psyche,* p. 110.
3. Author unknown. (1995). *Weight Watchers' Little Book of Wisdom.*
4. Stephen R. Covey. (1994). *Living the Seven Habits of Highly Effective People.*
5. Sun Tzu (Thomas Cleary, trans.). (1991). *The Art of War,* ch. 5, axiom 13, p. 35.

19

Initiation and Dedication

Maturity does not mean to become a captive of conceptualization. It is the realization of what lies in our innermost selves.

Bruce Lee, *Tao of Jeet Kune Do*

IT WAS NOT my intention to go into ritual theory and design in this work. This is a vast subject and deserves a book of its own. Yet I must discuss one aspect of ritual in this book—initiation. This is a foundation book; you've made a decision to take a new path. Such a decision deserves a rite of passage to mark the event. Initiation is that rite of passage.

Warriors involved in Wicca are already accessing the archetype of the Magickian. The Magickian is the master of knowledge and knowing. The Magickian uses this mastery to guide the processes of transformation. As such he is also an initiator. For it is the process of initiation that transforms us and others. The Warrior's path is a path of self-transformation.

As I pointed out in *Wiccan Warrior*, there is a connection between the life stages in the development of a person following the Wiccan

185

path and the three degrees of initiation. These stages and their corresponding degrees could be illustrated by looking at a typical, young, aspiring person who has studied and decided to dedicate himself to the Wiccan way of life. This is the true first degree—commitment. Later, having learned and matured, the Wiccan begins to assist others starting on this path, to teach, and to assume the role of a sister/brother/leader. This is the second degree. Finally the Wiccan enters the crone/elder phase, becoming an advisor for less senior Wiccans. This is the third degree. Many women view these "life stages" as Maiden, Mother, and Cronehood. However you label these life phases, you don't necessarily need an initiation to enter them.

Most denominations of Wicca have these three established degrees of initiation. Theoretically people studying one of these traditions will move upward until they arrive at the third and final degree. This then gives them the authority to go out and start a Coven of their own. Each degree entitles initiates to wear a particular color cord to designate their rank, the color varying between different traditions and Covens. This would be a familiar system to a student of the martial arts. Most martial arts schools have established grading systems through which a student must progress to become a master, marked by different colored belts.

Most martial arts schools using the degree system will tell you that a person must go through rigorous training and achieve certain training objectives before being passed on to the next level in that tradition. This is the primary justification for the degree system; it allows you to grade people according to the level of mastery of the knowledge required. But this practice is only about seventy years old. Originally all you got was a white belt. With wear, tear, and age it slowly turned brown, then black. By that time you were probably a master. Eventually the belt became frayed, loosening the threads and turning it white again. It was impatient people in the Western world who wanted grades as signposts to mark their progress.

Acquiring a degree or initiation is meaningless unless it really indicates a certain mastery has been attained. Through commitment, discipline, study, and hard work, one can achieve mastery in Wicca without ever having attended a Wiccan Circle or having ever received an "approved" initiation from any apostolic succession of clergy. If you haven't mastered your practice of Wicca, it doesn't matter how long an apostolic succession you have behind you.

I believe that Wicca is supposed to be a religion that allows us to find out what works for us, because we are all different. *Vive la différence!* You do not become a Witch by deciding to join some exclusive Wiccan clique. You become a Witch by making a decision to live as one. You join a Coven because it has attributes that complement your own and valuable lessons to offer you. It makes no difference whether it is part of an established tradition or not. The longest lasting Coven of my acquaintance was formed by a group of seekers who got together and read all they could on Wicca. They experimented. They all took turns as High Priest/ess and regularly practiced their craft.

In his book *Wicca: A Guide for the Solitary Practitioner,* Cunningham asked the question, "Who initiated the first Wiccan?"[1] With this question Cunningham reminds us that while the initiatory experience is a valuable one, it can be a solitary experience. In *The Triumph of the Moon,* Ronald Hutton pointed out that the majority of Wiccans out there are solitaries. Degrees are certainly not obligatory. Musashi, who trained himself, became a master swordsman who was never defeated. I'm reminded of the scene in the movie *The Karate Kid* where the young man asks his mentor what belt he has. The teacher looks at his belt and says, "J.C. Penney, $1.49." In the final analysis do all of those colored belts and certificates amount to much? Not very.

So why do an initiation at all? And what is an initiation anyway? Let's look at the following dictionary definition:

> **Initiate**, *v.t.;* initiated, *pt., pp.;* initiating, *ppr.* [from L. *initiatus, pp.* of *initiare,* to enter upon, initiate, from *initium,* a beginning.]
>
> 1. to bring into practice or use; to introduce by first doing or using.
>
> 2. to teach the fundamentals of some subject to; to help (someone) to begin doing something.
>
> 3. to admit as a member into a fraternity, club, etc., especially through use of secret ceremony or rites.
>
> **Syn.**—begin, commence, start, install, induct, inaugurate.
>
> *Initiatus, pp.* of *initiare,* to enter upon, initiate, from *initium,* a beginning.

Initiation *isn't* just a membership ceremony. You can experience an initiatory experience without the assistance of any group. The solitary vision quest of the First Nations Peoples of North America is just one example. You can experience a group initiatory experience such as the Greek Mysteries of Eleusis and not become a member of anything. Initiation is a rebirth, a beginning, entering into a new phase, striking out on a new adventure, setting out on a new path, like the Fool in the Tarot's Major Arcana. It is an individual experience, although several individuals can experience it in the same time and place. It brings about a change of consciousness. By this definition, the initiation ceremony must be created to facilitate this change in consciousness, this new beginning.

You can dedicate yourself to this Warrior's path all by yourself. Some religious systems make the initiatory experience a solitary one, setting up the conditions to allow the initiate to achieve her objective alone and unaided. That such initiations work is ample proof that much of the dogma surrounding institutionalized initiation ceremonies is largely unnecessary.

So if you have now decided that you wish to take this Warrior's path, you need some sort of right of passage to signal to the subconscious part of you that you've begun this new quest. This could be as simple as taking an oath. Such an oath may be more meaningful to you if you create it yourself. If you don't feel that creative just now, here is an example I crafted for myself.

Warrior's Admonition

My body is my temple: I will care for it.
I will not engage in useless activity.
I will listen to the Goddess.
I will help myself.
I will create my own reality.

My path is creativity: I will strive for it.
A serene path to enlightenment.
I will know myself.
I will master myself.
I will create my own reality.

I will nurture the ability to perceive the truth in all matters.
I will perceive that which cannot be seen with the eye.
I will learn from my mistakes.
I will teach myself.
I will create my own reality.

I will not be negligent, even in trifling matters.
Grace and guilt do not exist:
I will strive for responsibility.
I will honor myself.
I will create my own reality.

I will never disgrace the Goddess, the God, nor Wicca.
I will not harbor sinister designs.
I will harm none, do as I will.
I will master myself.
I will create my own reality.

Initiation in a Group Ritual

You may be the member of a Wiccan group and want to do a more elaborate rite of passage in a group ritual. I gave an example of an initiatory ritual that I designed for a male initiate in my previous book, *Wiccan Warrior*. The following Warrior rite of passage was written by Crystal Shadowmoon for her daughter Jade. Crystal graciously agreed to share it with you so that you could use it as an example in designing your own. Besides Crystal, the participants in this initiatory ritual were Delia Littlewing, Splash Eaglespirit, Kinder, Undine, Star, and Ananda. Comments by Crystal and Delia Littlewing are added to better describe what happened.

Jade's rite of passage was held during a Pagan camp-out in a wooded setting. As the mother of the child coming of age, Crystal felt that this rite would be more memorable if Jade was taken not just from her father, but from the community as well. Crystal was very anxious. "I felt like the mother of the bride," Crystal told me "I was terrified that something would go wrong."

Unfortunately things did go wrong at first. Crystal had spent all week sewing red tunics for the ceremony. When Crystal got to the campsite, she discovered that instead of bringing the tunics, she had brought a bag of red cloth. Crystal was devastated. At first she didn't know what to do. Then she accessed her Warrior spirit and decided to improvise.

"It's funny to think about it now," Crystal recalled. "The women (who had nothing to wear) stood around the campfire with a pair of scissors cutting this cloth into long strips. Our costumes turned out to be awesome! We tied strips of cloth around our tops to make a primitive-looking halter and another around our waist to make short skirts. The look? Very tribal." The women participating in this rite of passage painted tribal markings, or runes, on their faces with red ink and marks over their third eye. Some of them made up tribal arm bands. "We looked pretty hot in my opinion," Crystal recalled.

Jade's rite of passage began with a torchlit procession, drumming, and chanting. Only a few people knew that this rite would be taking place. To announce the beginning of Jade's rite, two criers were sent running through the camp, calling out in joyous tones that a child will be taken to become a woman. "They are coming for the child. They're coming to take the child! They're coming! The time is now!"

The unsuspecting festival participants were gathered around a big bonfire on the beach as the criers approached. "When we made our entrance, they stopped dead in their tracks," Crystal remembered. "The silence was disturbing. The people were standing there with their mouths open in surprise." Delia Littlewing reported that "we caught everyone totally off-guard. No one other than ourselves and our selected 'criers' knew to expect this. It was great. We had *impact*. . . . When we walked out to that river, everyone on the sandbar fell totally silent although they had been buzzing with curiosity and whispered questions just before we came around the bend."

As the group of initiators approached Jade, they chanted the Hecate Chant:

> Hecate, Cerridwen Dark Mother, take her in.
> Hecate, Cerridwen, let her be reborn.

Jade did not know that her rite of passage was to be that night. "My family and I went to a Pagan community camp out along with my Christian friend Kristen," Jade recalls, "On the night of my rite of passage, I was sitting around the campfire with Kristen and the new friends we made. My father came to join us (which surprised me because he's not Pagan either). When the crier came yelling, 'They are coming for the child,' I didn't know what to do because, in the back of my mind I knew he was talking about me. I had asked my mom for a rite of passage but I had no idea when she was going to do it. Now that it was time, I was shocked. I didn't know what to do or what to expect."

It was Crystal's job to invite Jade to participate in this rite of passage. As Crystal called to her daughter, her father and the criers protectively stepped in front of Jade. "We approached the child, challenged her to come, but left her with the choice," Delia Littlewing told me. "We told her we had to take her blindfolded, that she had to trust us to lead her through the forest to the isle of women. We warned her that she would be leaving her childhood behind and that she had to be prepared to accept the responsibilities that came with womanhood."

"We feel the time has come for you to become a woman," Crystal said to Jade. "Will you come?"

Crystal recalls that tears came to everyone's eyes when her father said, "Don't go, Jade. If you go, you will no longer be my little girl."

Again Crystal said, "Will you come?" Crystal held out her hand to Jade.

Jade looked at her father teary-eyed, then at Crystal and said, "Yes."

"When my mom came around the corner with all the women I had become close to, I was awestruck," Jade remembered. "They looked great! They asked me to come with them. I was a tad bit embarrassed but I followed. I was on my way to becoming a woman."

"I actually think that was the hardest decision she ever had to make," Crystal later recalled.

Once Jade agreed to come, Crystal asked Jade if she was coming in perfect love and perfect trust. When Jade said that she was, Crystal explained that Jade would be blindfolded as a symbol of her trust. Once Jade was blindfolded, the initiators led her away through narrow woodland trails. "It took a lot of trust for her to go with us on that long trek upriver blindfolded," Delia Littlewing recalled. "Across gullies and up and down embankments. We crossed the river twice, and all the while she stepped confidently at our direction and gentle nudges." As the women went, they chanted:

Snake woman shedding her skin,
Shedding, shedding, shedding her skin.

Still blindfolded, Jade was brought to sit by a small fire (the child's fire). Each woman then took a turn going to Jade to pass on words of wisdom. Crystal had told each of the participants that there was no limits on the wisdom that they could pass on to Jade. The first woman removed Jade's blindfold. Then, in turn, the various members of the group passed on advice concerning self-respect, inner strength and knowledge of yourself, spiritual growth, being self-reliant, womanhood, respect for others, and integrity. Crystal was the last to pass her daughter wisdom.

"During the ritual I was quiet at first because I was in complete shock and didn't know what to do," Jade recalled. "When the women passed on their knowledge to me, it really hit home. I feel that this was the most important part of the ritual. I would have never thought that I would need anyone to help me into woman-hood by talking to me about their past experiences. It seemed to me that you just grow breasts, turn eighteen, move out, and—*Poof!*—instant woman. But I learned that important things can be passed on from someone who has been through the things that you will definitely go through. My women ranged from the ages of twenty-three to fifty-five, and I learned a valuable lesson from each and every one of them. Although I will probably do all the things they warned me against and make the same mistakes that they did, their words will always be with me and at least I will be prepared to han-dle the situations. Another beautiful thing about being taught by them is that I know I can call anyone of them with a problem I may (and will) run into, and I will never hear 'I told you so.' All the women treated me like one of them that night and they still do. They never make me leave the room for confidential conversations or dirty jokes. As the ritual moved on, I loosened up a little (with a little help from the mugwort wine) and realized that I didn't have to be all stiff and unsure. All of these women are my friends, it's okay."

Following this, Jade was asked to remove her clothes. Crystal then washed Jade's forehead, hands, and feet in the stream. Jade was dressed in the red strips of cloth they had precut for her and then smudged with sage. Finally Jade was asked to join the women at the big fire. Seated before the big fire, Jade shared a mugwort wine made specially to facilitate visions with the women around her. Delia Littlewing presented her with the silver Chalice afterward.

Jade was asked if she had any unanswered questions about becoming a woman. "Finally she would be recognized as a woman, but this was not enough for the women who cherished her as a child," Crystal explained to me. "It was important to us that she not only be a woman, but a strong woman." The initiators discussed this with her a bit as they shared the Chalice of mugwort wine with her. The word "Warrior," however, was never mentioned.

The women drummed and sang Jade into an altered state, and then presented her with her challenge. They had hidden an axe and a shield in the woods, each one special. She had to venture into the dark forest alone to quest for them. This was her trial and her quest—to face her fears in unknown territory. While Jade went out on her quest, the women continued their chanting and drumming.

After Jade returned with her treasures, the initiators prevented her from re-entering the Circle around the fire.

"Are you a woman or a Warrior?" she was asked. The plan was that if Jade had answered incorrectly, the next person would ask her the same question, and so on until Jade got it right. Of course, the correct answer should be "Both." Jade answered correctly on the first attempt.

The initiators then allowed Jade into the sacred space. The initiators painted Jade with clay. The quarters were called and the Circle cast. Each woman then called a Goddess to protect Jade, guide her, and witness the rite. Crystal recalls that most of the women called a Dark Goddess. "It just seemed so appropriate," Crystal told me later. Crystal called upon the Morrighan:

> I call upon the Morrighan, the Dark Goddess, the Triple Crone. I stand before you and ask that you grace us with your presence tonight. I ask you to bless and protect this child, Jade, and bestow upon her the gifts of wisdom and strength as she puts aside her childhood and begins a new journey as a woman. Grace her with the knowledge of your presence, Show her the wisdom of your mysteries and lead her to the path of strength and integrity. So mote it be!

The initiators then asked Jade to show them her treasures. Crystal explained to Jade that the axe represented her psychic offense and the shield represented her psychic defense:

> This is no ordinary axe. Look at it closely. This a gift from the Goddess herself. This ax represents your psychic offense. It will be your ally in battle. You must give your weapon a name that is known only to you and the Goddess. This will empower your weapon and allow you to call upon it's strength whenever you feel the need to protect yourself. Hold your weapon up to the Goddess and silently give it a name now. Remember, you must choose your battles wisely. Never use your gift maliciously. Its purpose is for warding off attacks only.
>
> This is no ordinary shield. This shield represents your psychic defense. It will also be your ally in battle. You must also give your shield a secret name. Again this will empower your shield and allow only you to call upon its power. Name your shield now.

Each woman presented Jade with a heartfelt gift to attach to her shield. Crystal's gift was a wolf symbol. As she presented it, Crystal told her daughter:

> I give you the gifts of the wolf. The wolf has the ability to pass by danger invisibly, outwitting those who wish them

harm, fighting when necessary. The wolf will lead you to a spiritual teacher. The wolf is also known for wisdom, hunting and seeking, magick, dreams, transformation and protection.

Splash then presented Jade with a beautiful necklace as a symbol of courage, and a matching bracelet as a symbol of honor. Splash spoke a few words on what it means to be a Warrior.

Jade then had to take an oath:

Do you promise to defend yourself and protect yourself?

When all of this was done the women challenged Jade to dedicate herself to the Goddess as both a woman and a Warrior in her own words. She had to acknowledge her strength and power. She promised to defend those who are afraid to defend themselves.

Finally Jade had to chose a Warrior name for herself that would only been known to those in this Circle. Jade walked around the Circle three times while the women chanted her new name. The women then chanted, "You are a strong woman, you are a story woman, you are a healer, your soul will never die," until Jade joined in and sang with conviction, "I am a strong woman, I am a story woman, I am a healer, My soul will never die!" The Circle concluded following a ceremony of cakes and wine.

The women escorted Jade down the long trek back to the river to rejoin the community back on the beach singing, "Blossom woman opening wide, opening, opening wide." Jade was now tattooed and dressed in the same red garments as the other women. Jade was presented to the community as a woman and a Warrior. Jade remained at the fire, reveling in her new status in the community, celebrating her rite of passage.

"Maybe I'm just a proud mother, but her dedication was beautiful and it definitely came from a woman," Crystal told me. "We were all very shocked to discover that we were definitely between the worlds. What seemed to take an hour had actually lasted for four hours! It was very powerful. We all received something on that night. It was the strongest Circle I had ever been in, and most of the other women agreed. After it was over, we were approached by several people who watched us take her away. They all thanked us for letting them be part of Jade's rite of passage. They told us it was very powerful from the start and they felt privileged to be witnesses of this important event."

"We went on with the ritual for what seemed to be about an hour but was actually about four," Jade remembered. "I returned to the community a woman that night and I still get the respect of a woman from everyone around me. It truly was a wonderful experience that every Pagan child should have the privilege of." Note that all of the people involved participated in this ritual to some extent or other. They took part in the procession, they chanted, they offered gifts. The whole group shared the energetic experience. Each woman was allowed to call on what aspects of deity they wished and to offer what advice they felt appropriate. This promoted spontaneity and creativity. Note how Crystal incorporated the quest into Jade's experience, emphasizing that this ritual was simply allowing Jade to initiate herself. This was the ordeal that had to be overcome to enter into the new phase.

In this chapter we've examined dedications and initiations. It is appropriate that this last example of ritual should incorporate symbolic Magickal Weapons. In the next chapter we will examine some other Magickal Weapons, the Sword and the Athame.

Endnote

1. Scott Cunningham. (1988). *Wicca: A Guide for the Solitary Practitioner,* p. 73.

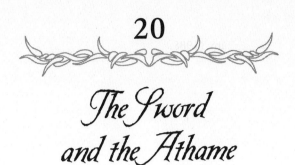

20

The Sword
and the Athame

When valour preys on reason,
It eats the sword it fights with.

William Shakespeare, *Antony and Cleopatra*

SWORDS FIRST BECAME differentiated from daggers in the Bronze Age (about 3000 B.C.E.). Edged weapons of this sort aren't long-distance weapons like spears and arrows; they are close-quarter weapons. Throughout history, combatants have used cutting and stabbing weapons such as swords and daggers to control the area within their reach.

Most Wiccans carry a dagger called an Athame in Circle, though some Wiccans prefer to carry a Wand instead. Usually there is only one Sword in a Wiccan Circle. This Sword is used by whoever is directing the ritual. Athames are double-edged daggers. Using such Magickal Weapons is a double-edged proposition.

Of all of the Magickal Weapons found in a Wiccan Circle, the Athame and the Sword are the ones that are most obviously weapons. As I have pointed out in previous books, much is made of the fact that Wiccans carry such ritual Weapons in Circle. A cop

199

sent to investigate a Pagan group doing an outdoor ritual is immediately going to focus on such ritual tools; out of habit he is looking for anything that might be used as a weapon. The average passersby will see these edged weapons and be reminded of the sensational and inaccurate media hype about secret ceremonies and sacrifices. The questions and media attention have, in the past, lead to numerous public relations headaches. In countless how-to books of magick and ritual I've seen disclaimers about ritual knives. They often recommend using less-obvious everyday items such as letter openers or kitchen knives as Athames.

There have been other problems besides these public relations nightmares. I've received many requests for help from people across the continent who have had their ritual knives confiscated by airport security or customs agents. It is interesting that one of the first things that happened when word got around that I was both a cop and Wiccan was that I was bombarded by letters from prison inmates. These prisoners wanted me to write to their warden to tell him that as they were Wiccan, they could have a knife in jail. I'm sure that most of the people who wrote me weren't really Wiccans; they were just cons looking for another way to scam the system. There have even been people before the courts who have tried to defend their carrying of concealed knives by claiming that Wiccans carry Athames everywhere (Athames aren't Sikh *kirpans,* we don't carry Athames outside of ritual).

As I mentioned in chapter 7, the ritual use of Magickal Weapons such as the Sword or Athame is a practice that we borrowed from Ceremonial Magick. Ceremonial magickians brandished daggers toward the quarters of the Circle in an attempt to force external entities and energies to comply with their wishes. These magickians carry magick Swords as a form of protection against these external forces. These customs are a part of a Judeo-Christian magickal system that treats energy and divinity as separate from humankind. They are customs from a system that seeks domination of the Earth's forces.

As a Wiccan, I reject this external system. I am a steward of universal energy. My power does not come from domination, it comes from mastery. My Circle is designed to hold in the energy that I raise. I don't need edged weapons to protect me from spirits. I don't want the energy outside of the Circle I create; I want the energy to flow through me and the Circle.

Another place that the Athame or Sword appears in Wiccan ritual is in initiation ceremonies. In some traditions, the blindfolded novice is challenged at the entrance to the Circle by a Covener brandishing an edged weapon. The point is pressed against the novice's chest and he is challenged:

> O thou who standest on the threshold between the pleasant world of men and the dread domains of the Lords of the Outer Spaces, hast thou the courage to make the assay? For I say verily, it were better to rush upon my blade and perish, than make the attempt with fear in thy heart.[1]

This is another clear example of how Gardner viewed the Athame—as a Magickal Weapon. It is a perfect example of an attempt to instill fear into the heart of the initiate through threats of violence with an edged weapon. This isn't the sort of thing that one expects to find on a nonviolent Wiccan path. It is a custom borrowed from Freemasonry, and I think that it is high time we discarded it. If we are bringing this person into a community of love and trust, how can we justify such an action? How can you enter a Circle in perfect love and trust if someone has just threatened you? You'll notice that Crystal didn't incorporate this into Jade's Warrior Rite of Passage that we examined in the previous chapter. Crystal devised an ordeal to test the initiate that did not depend on such a device.

So let me remind you of the seventh Warrior Precept: *Minimal appearance, maximum content.* Appearances can be deceptive. It isn't the tools that make you powerful. They are just extensions of yourself. If you haven't achieved the mastery of yourself, then these extensions won't be extending your abilities very far. I don't run into the problem of customs and airport security because I don't take an Athame with me to festivals and rituals. I don't really need it.

I do not mean to say that these edged Magical Weapons of Air do not have any ritual or magickal purpose at all. As I pointed out earlier, Wiccans traditionally use Swords or Athames to cast a Circle. One of the reasons for this is that, as they walk the perimeter of the Circle with the Sword, they are symbolically cutting themselves off from the mundane world. These Weapons of Air pierce between the worlds, separating the sacred space from everyday reality. The edge of the Weapon of Air defines the edge of the sacred space in the mind of the participants. This is a powerful symbolic act. This can be especially effective in large group situations where the use of such symbolism is necessary to put all of the participants "on the same page." It is a ritual gesture that everyone can see and understand. A similar process occurs when the Athame is used to "cut a door" in the Circle to allow participants to pass freely in and out. The edge of the Weapon is defining the edge of the portal in the mind of the participants.

The more important purpose of the Athame or Sword is as a focussing tool. In this they are very similar to the Weapons of Fire (Wand and the Spear or Staff). Double-edged blades seem to do a better job of focussing energy than single-edged blades. This is probably because their structure is more symmetrical. It is best if your Athame or Sword has a grip made of natural materials such as wood, leather, or bone. Even a metal grip is acceptable. The reason for this is that such handles do not impede the flow of chi from you to the blade. Handles made of artificial materials such as rubber, plastic, or fiberglass have less conductivity, and may impede the flow of chi.

For an Athame, the blade should be about the length of your hand (six to eight inches). For a Sword, the length of the blade should be about the length of your forearm.

As edged weapons are used to stab and thrust, it is natural to think of them as phallic tools that project energy. Yet any serious student of the sword forms in Asian martial arts will tell you that the Sword is used to draw energy *into* you. As the double-edged sword can cut in either direction, so can the energy flow through it in either direction. In this, the Sword is very like the Wand. Here is that receptive/projective principle that we encountered earlier in chapter 6. The Weapons of Air are focussing tools—like the Weapons of Fire, you can use them to focus the chi both inward and outward.

It doesn't really matter which hand you hold the Athame in. Remember I told you earlier that you can (and should) learn to send and receive energy through either hand. The Sword is only different in that it is bigger. Holding it two-handed gives you the ability to channel energy in and out through both of your hands at once.

The Sword or Athame can be used as a focussing tool in a similar fashion to the Wand. The same techniques apply. Try the Lifting the Sky exercise for the Wand that you learned in chapter 16 with an Athame or Sword instead of a Wand. See how each of these tools feels to you using this technique. Try sending chi out and drawing chi in. Record your impressions in your Book of Shadows. If you have trouble visualizing the flow of energy through your Wand, try the hand-squeezing exercise you learned for the Wand. Let the chi flow down your arm as the tension in it dissolves. As this wave of energy reaches your hand it will stream through the Athame.

In this chapter you've learned the significance and use of the Sword and Athame. You've learned some additional magickal techniques involving cords. All that remains in this book is to examine the Magick and the Seasons of Air.

Endnote

1. Janet Farrar and Stewart Farrar. (1984). *A Witches Bible*, Volume II: The Rituals, p. 17.

21

The Magick and Seasons of Air

Rough winds do shake the darling buds of May.

William Shakespeare, *Sonnet 18*

THE MAGICK OF Air is primarily the magick of sound energy. This sort of magick can effectively be used both in a solitary setting and as a group. Let's look at some techniques of Air magick.

Mantras and Toning

One of the ways of sharing group energy this way is through the use of mantras. The word "mantra" comes from a Sanskrit root, which means to "think or reason." This is usually taken to mean verbalizing such thought. Any sound or combination of sounds could become a mantra. This is related to the ancient idea that knowing the correct name for a thing gives you power over it. This is a vital part of the concept of mantras—once you know the real name of a thing, you can create it by its sound.

This is the reasoning behind the ancient Hebrew prohibitions about speaking aloud the name of their God, usually rendered in Hebrew as YHVH, also known as the Tetragrammaton, a word

205

that literally translates as "four-letter word." It was because of this prohibition that the Hebrews used corruptions of the pronunciation such as "Yahweh," which later became "Jehovah." There are myths all over the world concerning deities who got in trouble because their real name was somehow revealed or because they swore by their name and therefore couldn't evade their oath.

The German jazz historian Joachim Ernst-Berendt once said, "a) since the one sure thing we can say about fundamental matter is that it is vibrating and, b) since all vibrations are theoretically sound, then c) it is not unreasonable to suggest that the universe is music and should be perceived as such."[1] The magickal power of song is a very old concept. A mythical example of this magickal power of words in song is in the epic Finnish poem, the *Kalevala*. In it the God Väinämöinen transforms Joukahainen, who had angered him, into part of the landscape simply by singing.

In Tantra, there is a principle called *varna,* which holds that sound is eternal and that every letter of the alphabet is a deity. Words become words of power. You can see something like this in Cabalistic numerology systems, which assign power to each letter of the Hebrew alphabet, although they don't take it quite this far. There is a parallel in the Norse Runes and their interpretations as well. This is also the basis of the ceremonial magickian's grimoires. A grimoire is a list of words and names of power.

Related to this Tantric concept is the theory that every entity has a sound which creates it out of the void—a "germ" sound (in the sense of germination). The Hindus call this germ sound *nada* and consider it to be the heart of creation. One example is the well-known mantra usually written as "OM," which is actually the triphthong "AUM." The *A* stands for *Agni,* or fire, and is also related to the god Vishnu. *U* stands for *Varuna,* or water, and is also related to Shiva. The *M* stands for *Marut,* or air, and is related to Brahma. Thus, by chanting "AUM" you are invoking this trinity of deities.

In Eastern philosophy, mantras can take the form of single phrases, called *dharanis.* Sometimes they are called *satya-vacana,* which refers to the solemn uttering of a great truth. An example of using a dharani to invoke deities is the chant used by the Krishna Consciousness movement. It goes like this, "Hare Krishna, Hare Krishna, Krishna, Krishna, Hare Hare; Hare Rama, Hare Rama, Rama Rama, Hare, Hare." Hare means "Hail" and Krishna and Rama are deities in the Hindu pantheon.

Lest you think that this concept is foreign to Western culture, just look at the practices of the Christian church. Common mantras in Catholic churches include choruses of "Hallelujah," Hail Marys, and the well-known phrase, "In the Name of the Father, and of the Son, and of the Holy Spirit." By saying these words, Catholics expect to invoke this power. But of course, as many a Catholic theologian will tell you, there is no magick in Catholicism!

In modern Wicca, chanting, toning, and song are modern terms for these old concepts of mantra and dharani. In toning, a single syllable sound is repeatedly sung to raise energy. Toning stimulates the flow of energy in you. By using the proper mantras, the Wiccan Warrior can raise the type of energy needed so that he can send it to where it is needed. Different mantras have different effects.

For example, try toning the well-known mantra "AUM" for a few minutes. Notice how it draws energy inward. Now try the mantra "MA" (pronounced as in "grandMA"). Notice how the energy is now flowing out from you. The first would obviously be most useful if you are trying to recharge your depleted energy at the end of a trying day. The latter would be more useful if you were trying to send healing energy to somebody else.

Another mantra that can energize you is the sound "HA." Take three sharp breaths in and then shout "HA!" Do this a few times and see how you feel. It is a very useful technique if you find your reserves depleted. The shout or *kiai* or *heit* that accompanies a punch or kick in martial arts such as Karate is actually this mantra. If uttered at the moment of contact, it helps to release the chi. In Kendo, calls known as *katsu* are used with upward stabbing moves and calls known as *totsu* with striking motions. Ever noticed how a weightlifter will yell while completing an especially heavy lift? It's the same principle at work.

One mantra that can relax you is called "Bhramari breathing." Sit in a comfortable position. Begin making a soft snoring sound as you exhale (with practice you can make this sound while inhaling too). It does not have to be loud; it should sound like a sigh or a groan. Start with a low pitch and with each breath raise it an octave until it feels right to you. Continue until you feel like making a big sigh. It takes about twenty exhalations to arrive at this point. This big sigh signals that the exercise has worked.

Bhramari breathing will slow your breathing and heart rate quite rapidly. This works partly because it mimics snoring, a sound you usually make while asleep. This triggers the same sort of relaxation response in your waking consciousness. This is a very useful technique that the Wiccan Warrior can use to reduce stress. Bhramari breathing can also be used to eliminate pain, and is especially effective to relieve migraines. In Chi Kung it is recognized that softly blowing on a wound while making a hissing "shsss" sound can reduce the pain of the wound. Bhramari breathing also has a healing effect. Frequencies between 20 to 50 Hz have been found to strengthen human bones and help them grow. This is the frequency range in which cats purr, which may account for why they seem to have remarkable powers of recuperation.[2]

Toning can easily be used in a group setting. Get the group to stand or sit in a circle, facing inward. Partipicants take a deep breath and then sing the chosen tone until they run out of breath. They then quickly take another breath and repeat the tone. Because different people are running out of breath at different times, the sound of the group's mantra should be more or less continuous. Start with a low pitch. As each person feels the energy start to rise, they raise their voice an octave in pitch, or increase the volume. All watch the person directing the group. This leader will use some sort of agreed signal like raising her arms to indicate when the energy has peaked. Like with Bhramari breathing, this will occur at a point where the tone sounds and feels "right." When the signal is given, all of the participants stop toning and direct the energy raised to wherever it is required.

You should create a section in your Book of Shadows on "Toning." Record these toning sessions in this section; list the objectives, the tone used, your impressions, and the results. This will help you keep track of which tones work best for you (and your group).

A variation of this technique is commonly used to send group energy for healing or achieving some objective directly to one of the group members. For example, a person could use this if they needed extra energy for inspiration in finding a job. The person to whom the energy is being sent stands in the middle of a circle formed by the other members of the Coven. The members in the surrounding circle may lift their arms to point their palms toward the person in the middle to help direct the energy. The group does toning, using an appropriate mantra. One effective technique is to use the name of the person in the middle of their Circle as the mantra. If they wish, they may alternate this with simple words representing the person's desire. In the example given above, the words "success," "employment," or "abundance" would be appropriate. When the energy peaks, the participants stop toning and direct the energy to the person in the middle. They may actually touch the person if they wish. This is a very powerful experience for the person in the middle, surrounded by friends invoking him or her by name. It is particularly effective to improve a person's self-image and confidence. Have the group do this for you and record your impressions in your Book of Shadows. If you don't belong to a group, try toning your own name.

In the Book of Fire you learned techniques such as the Cone of Power to project energy long distance both individually and with a group. Toning mantras is a particularly effective technique to raise a Cone of Power. As I mentioned in my description of Bhramari breathing, you tone until the tone "feels right" to you. At this point what you need to do to create a Cone of Power is to release the energy outward toward your magickal objective. Imagine the energy streaming out of the Circle with your objective at the apex of the Cone.

Raising energy through toning is a bit like performing jazz music. Everyone contributes to the total experience. Some groups have trouble raising energy through singing and chanting—the participants are self-conscious or lack musical ability. If you are working with a group of people like this, toning can make it a lot easier for you.

Raising Energy Through Drumming

The ecstatic use of the drum is not a part of mainstream religion in modern Western culture. Yet percussion is one of the world's oldest forms of music and one of the most powerful ways to raise energy. War drums, like the Celtic bodhran, used to be very well-known to the Warrior. Percussion instruments were the first and are among the most powerful musical instruments in our possession. "Percussion was almost universally used during such rituals of transition as birth, puberty, marriage, and death, when the spirit world is called upon for guidance."[3]

Anyone who has ever witnessed a performance by troupes of Japanese Taiko drummers, like Za Ondekoza or Kodo, cannot fail to have experienced the electrifying energy that they raise in each performance. These troupes don't just drum, they *live* drumming. They live communally, eating pure foods, drumming and meditating as much as fifteen or sixteen hours a day. It is living a spiritual life with the central path to enlightenment being the drumming.

In fact, Za Odekoza ("Demon Drummers") is as good an example of a troupe of Warriors as you are likely to find. They were founded by Tagayasu Den on Sado Island in Japan in 1969. They prepared themselves through rigorous physical training in marathon running and the art of Taiko, the giant Japanese barrel drums. In 1975 they amazed the world by crossing the finish line of the Boston Marathon and immediately running to the stage to perform. Between 1990 and 1993 they performed in 355 cities the U.S., running from one city to the next between performances. One day they ran 64.64 km. They wore out 121 pairs of shoes and averaged two dollars per day for meals. Such was their dedication.

In India, apprentice drummers seclude themselves in huts for up to forty days in a retreat called a *Chilla.* All they do while they are in the hut is drum. Within a few days they have all manner of visions. Shamans the world over "ride" the sound of their drums into other dimensions. Other religious traditions, such as Voudoun or Santería, use drumming to summon spirits or gods down into someone other than the drummer, usually a dancer. In Voudoun these spirits are known as *Loa,* and are said to "ride" the dancers.

Drumming has an amazing effect on human consciousness. In 1665, Dutch scientist Christian Huygens discovered what is now known as the law of entrainment. This law holds that if two rhythms are nearly the same, and their sources are in close proximity, they will always tend to synchronize or "entrain." It is believed that this is because it takes less energy to synchronize than to pulse in opposition to one another. Psychologist Andrew Neher "found that he could 'drive' or 'entrain' the brain waves of his experimental subjects down into what is called the alpha/theta border, meaning that a majority of the electrical activity in their brains was pulsing at a rate of between six and eight cycles per second."[4] The alpha/theta state is the state that occurs just outside the delta, or sleep, state in which visions occur.

The percussion of drumming activates the root chakra, or Muladhara. This is one of the reasons that people find the heavy beat of music in night clubs so appealing—the beat activates Mulhadara, the root chakra, sending the kundalini energy rising up the chakras inside them.

The Wiccan Warrior can recapture the motivational and meditation power of the drum known to our forebears. It's also an excellent way of lowering your stress levels and raising energy. Any type of drum will suffice—a simple frame drum, djembe or dumbec, bongos, congas, you name it.

Drum trancing is not difficult to achieve. Take your drum and start quietly. Gradually build the volume and tempo to help move the energy. If you are chanting a mantra in conjunction with your drumming, make sure that the beat of the drum matches the cadence of the mantra. After your drumming session, record your impressions in your Book of Shadows.

Cord Magick

There is a long history of the use of cords in Wiccan magick. I include them in the Book of Air because they mostly involve use of the Athame. Cords are for binding, and the Weapons of Air are for separating things: *this* from *that*. For example, the Athame is placed in the ground at the center of the Circle and one end the cord is attached to it. The cord is then used as a sort of compass to trace out the perimeter of the Circle.

Like candle magick, the color of the cords you use can be chosen to represent the aspects of your magickal objective. Different colors invoke different emotions and feelings, which we can put to use in our magick. This is helpful in designing and enhancing your magick. You can refer to the list of color that you made earlier in your Book of Shadows for the attributes that relate to your magick (if you haven't made this list yet, see chapter 11).

One technique you can use to help you eliminate habits, or detach yourself from persons or habits that may be holding you back, is cord cutting. You take a number of cords or strings, each representing an aspect or person involved. One end of each you tie to some object—it could be the altar, a tree, a candle stand, whatever. The other ends you hold in one hand. As you visualize these strings as representing the bonds holding you back, you take your Athame and, one by one, cut the cords. In your mind, see these bonds fall away from you, setting you free. The Athame or Sword is a symbol of the magickian's will. In this case you are using your will to cut away the impediments in your life.

This cord-cutting magick is another example of how the cords and the Athame are used together. This is also a form of initiation. It is a symbolic Rite of Passage that helps your mind separate itself from whatever impedes it.

Cord braiding is a technique that helps you to focus on your magickal objective. As a focussing tool, it is similar to the use of prayer beads or rosaries. Take three equal lengths of cord, side by side. At one end tie the three cords together. You can then secure this end to your Athame, which you stick in the ground in front of you. You could also use some sort of anchor, like a chair or table, or have another person hold this end while you work. The object of this form of magic is to visualize the successful accomplishment of your magical goal while you braid (or knot) the cords.

With each new knot or braid, you think of another aspect of your objective. You can actually speak these thoughts out loud as you do each braid or knot, if you like. The longer the cords that you use, the more likely it is that you will have to repeat yourself. You may have to think long and hard to think of additional things to visualize or voice, and that is the secret behind this form of magick. It forces you to focus on what you are doing and constantly come up with new ideas about your objective, thus increasing your concentration on the task at hand.

As always, record your impressions and results in your Book of Shadows. This will help you to monitor your progress and identify problems if things don't work out quite right.

Some people tie the knots in a particular order and even recite rhymes with each knot tied. An example is, "One, the spell's begun/Two, my words are true/Three, it comes to be, etc." I find that it is far more important and effective to focus on the objective of the magick being worked than to try to remember the next line in some cute poem or what order to tie the knots in.

Seasons of Air

In ancient times, this season was a time of mobilization. It was the time of year when Warriors were called to service from their winter quarters. This is when Warriors commence work on the resolutions and plans made in the Seasons of Earth. The Seasons of Air are seasons of beginnings. This is the time of year when I convert the plans I have made in the Seasons of Earth into action. For, as the old proverb says, "the shortest answer is doing."[5]

Imbolc is the Greater Sabbat that occurs on February 2. Imbolc is the date by which I put my plans and resolutions into effect. It is a time of beginnings and consecration. It is a time of commitment. It is a time for doing magick for success. The time for making resolutions is over—it is time to get to work, for "a thought which does not result in an action is nothing much."[6] As Imbolc is the time when the first signs of the returning spring begin to appear, it is the time when your projects should start to take shape. This is when you plant the magickal seed that will grow into the object of your desires. Imbolc was when I chose the title for this work and began making the notes that would outline its structure.

Eostre is the Lesser Sabbat that marks the Spring equinox. Eostre is a fertile time when I am working hard on my projects. For the Warrior it is a time to realize the fertile ideas and concepts that were conceived during the Seasons of Earth. This is where I water and nurture the magickal seed of the idea that I planted. As the project evolves, I can begin to see the shape and direction it is taking on. Eostre was the time when I started writing the chapters of this work in earnest. This was when I began to fully realize what I was creating.

The Seasons of Air are seasons of beginnings. This is the symbolism of the eastern quadrant of the Circle. Now that I have taken you through the elements and seasons, it is time for you to begin your Warrior journey.

Endnotes

1. Mickey Hart. (1990). *Drumming at the Edge of Magic,* p. 119.
2. David Harrison. (2001). "Cats' Purring Linked to Old Wives' Tale of Their Nine Lives," *National Post,* Tuesday, March 20, 2001.
3. Mickey Hart. (1990). *Drumming at the Edge of Magic,* p. 112.
4. Ibid., p. 114.
5. English proverb. Collected in George Herbert's *Jacula Prudentum* (1651).
6. Georges Bernanos. (1955). *The Last Essays of Georges Bernanos,* "France Before the World of Tomorrow."

Conclusion

The profession of magician is one of the most perilous and arduous specialisations of the imagination. On the one hand there is the hostility of God and the police to be guarded against; on the other it is as difficult as music, as deep as poetry, as ingenious as stage-craft, as nervous as the manufacture of high explosives, and as delicate as the trade in narcotics.

William Bolitho, "Twelve Against the Gods"

I'VE BROUGHT YOU widdershins through the elements and seasons to the east of the Circle, the place of the rising sun, the place of beginnings. This symbolizes where you now are. This is a place of beginnings for you. This is where your Warrior's path really starts, at the end of this work. You've served your apprenticeship. Our widdershins journey has hopefully helped to banish the negative elements from your life and left you the freedom to take charge of your life.

Here are the Warrior Precepts you have learned:

1. *Know thyself.*

2. *Nurture the ability to perceive the truth in all matters.*

217

3. *You create your own reality.*

4. *Develop a sense of Right Action.*

5. *Do not be negligent, even in trifling matters.*

6. *Your body is your temple—care for it!*

7. *Minimal appearance, maximum content.*

8. *Perceive that which cannot be seen with the eye.*

9. *Power with.*

10. *Who dares wins.*

11. *The Gods cannot help those who will not help themselves.*

12. *Be creative!*

13. *Do not engage in useless activity.*

You've learned that you are connected to the natural world through the five elements of Spirit, Air, Fire, Water, and Earth. This energy flows through you. You've discovered that this elemental energy can be enclosed and magnified by the five sides of the Witch's Pyramid:

1. *To Know*—Developing a complete understanding of the situation.

2. *To Keep Silent*—Making your mind still, so that your awareness can encompass your situation and give you this understanding.

3. *To Dare*—To make the decision to use your magickal power to take charge of your situation.

4. *To Imagine*—To clearly visualize your magickal objective.

5. *To Will*—To take the energy that you've raised and direct it unerringly at your goal.

With these five principles, you can overcome anything. This is what magick is all about.

Each of these five elements and sides is symbolized in a pair of Magickal Weapons. You've listed these in your Book of Shadows and discovered that the greatest of them is the pair of Mind and Spirit, for these control them all. You should now be able to see how all of the elements, cardinal points and concepts of the Witch's Pyramid work together. One way of looking at this is to think of yourself as a sort of "magickal artillery." In this model:

◆ Center / Spirit / *To Know*—This is the base that you operate off of, the axis mundi.

◆ North / Earth / *To Keep Silent*—This is the meditative process that brings magickal energy in and "loads" you up.

◆ West / Water / *To Dare*—This is the process that builds up the emotional pressure to send the magickal energy on its way.

◆ South / Fire / *To Imagine*—This is the meditative process that allows you to "aim" the magickal energy by visualizing the objective.

◆ East / Air / *To Will*—This is the "trigger" that sends the energy out and directs it on to its objective.

From this book, hopefully you've learned that all that you need to succeed magickally in this world is what you were born with. What you have to do is master what you've already got, to overcome adversity and reach for the stars. Magick is your birthright. The energy is already there, you just have to put it to use. You are the master of your own fate. Master yourself and everything else will be taken care of.

By this point you should have the beginnings of a Book of Shadows that is a true working journal. It includes your personal inventory of characteristics that is your primary "toolbox." It records the impressions from your dreaming and your meditation. It documents the results of the various magickal techniques that you've experimented with. It won't be just another published Book of Shadows that you bought in some bookstore. It won't be like any Book of Shadows that you transcribed word-for-word from somebody else's. It will not be like any other Book of Shadows in the universe. That is how it should be, because you are unique in this universe, too. Your Book of Shadows is special, just like you.

Apart from initiation, I haven't said much about ritual in this work. As I said earlier, that is such a large subject it deserves a book to itself. I think the mistake that many people make when they first come to Wicca is that they dive into the ritual and celebratory stuff before they understand the use of energy. This is a foundation book. In it I wanted to focus on the principles of magick and energy use that should form the basis of your Wiccan path.

This does not mean that you should not be recording ritual in your Book of Shadows. I encourage you to record the rituals you have experienced in this working journal. This will help you to develop ideas for your own rituals in the future.

Making a decision to travel down this Warrior path may not seem that big a step in your life right now. Only once you have achieved some of the objects of your desires with this new-found power will you fully appreciate what you have done here. The Swiss philosopher Henri-Frédéric Amiel said that "what we call little things are merely the causes of great things; they are the beginning, the embryo, and it is the point of departure which, generally speaking, decides the whole future of an existence. One single black speck may be the beginning of a gangrene, of a storm, of a revolution."[1] Historian Golo Mann once said:

Man is always more than he can know of himself; conse-quently, his accomplishments, time and again, will come as a surprise to him.[2]

You are more than you realize yourself to be. You can achieve your dreams. All you have to do is reach for them. This is what being a Wiccan Warrior is all about. Face your fears and go forward. Be glorious!

Endnotes

1. Henri-Frédéric Amiel. (1882; trans. by Mrs. Humphry Ward, 1892). *Journal Intime,* entry for 16 March 1868.

2. Golo Mann. (1987: tr. 1989). Quoted in Marcel Reich-Ranicki, *Thomas Mann and His Family,* "Golo Mann—The Liberation of an Unloved One."

Glossary

THE FOLLOWING IS a short list of common Wiccan terms, listing their derivation and use.

Altar: A table, stone, or other surface used in rituals on which the ritual tools are placed. Originally it was thought that this derived from the Latin word *altus* ("high"), but this is no longer generally accepted. This word first appeared in Old English around 1000 C.E. It came from the Latin *altaria* and *altare,* which in turn came from the Sanskrit *alata-m* ("firebrand"). Its root word is the Indo-European *al* ("burn"). This is in reference to the candles or offerings found burning on an altar. In John Dee's Enochian system of magic the altar was called the "holy table" or "table of practice." The altar used by the Hermetic Order of the Golden Dawn is black, symbolizing their intention to separate the Philosophic Gold from Matter, whose symbol is the black dragon. The Golden Dawn used the symbol of the Altar of Burnt Offering to represent the Qlippoth, or Evil. In Wiccan the altar is normally situated slightly north of the center of the Circle.

Anointing: (1) Another term for Wiccaning (see *Wiccaning*); (2) Preparing a candle for candle magick by applying scented substances to the candle.

Athame: The Wiccan's traditional consecrated, black-handled knife. The Athame is the Lesser Magickal Weapon of Air, the Greater one being the Sword. In most Wiccan traditions, each Coven member will carry an Athame, although some traditions will substitute Wands.

The Athame is a magical tool which first appears with the name *arthame* in French transcripts of the Greater Key of Solomon (specifically manuscript number 2350 in the Bilbioteque de l'Arsenal in Paris, titled *Le Secret des secrets, autrement la Clavicule de Salomon ou le veritable Grimoire*).[1] In De Givry's *Witchcraft, Magic and Alchemy,* the "arthame" is described as being the magic knife of the Witch.[2] A tool with a similar name, an "arctrave" or hook, appears in the *Book of True Black Magic,* which is based on the *Greater Key of Solomon.*[3] Sybil Leek refers to it as an "athalme." Similar terms include "athamas," a variation of the Greek word *Athanatos* ("immortal") used in the consecration of the sacred pen in the *Greater Key of Solomon* and "athemay," the name of the sun in summer in Barrett's *The Magus.*

Doreen Valiente points out that Clark Aston Smith introduced the arthame as a tool of magick with the name "Athame" in his story, "The Master of the Crabs," which appeared in the magazine *Weird Tales* in 1947. Valiente also points out that: "some present day exponents of the near-eastern cult of Sufism have attributed it to the Arabic 'adh-dhame,' meaning 'blood letter,' in the sense of it being a shedder of blood, which is just what the witches' Athame is not."[4] Valiente then dismisses the Sufist theory of the word's origins for this reason.

Now while the Athame is definitely *not* used to draw blood in modern Wiccan practice, we cannot say that this is alone is a valid reason to reject the possibility that this was, in fact, the original root of this word. Walker reports that the name of this Moorish-Arab-Andalusian weapon was the *al-dhamme,* which was used by a cult of moon worshippers called the "Double Horned-ones." It was called the "blood letter" because it was used in a ritual scarring ceremony.[5]

As an aside, the closest word that I could find in English is the Middle English *anlace,* or *anelace,* also known as an *anglas* in Welsh, which was a broad, tapering knife or dagger, from eighteen to twenty-four inches in length, and which was worn at the waist.

Baculum: A Wand used in Wiccan rituals (see *Wand*). This term is derived from *baculus,* a Latin term meaning "staff" or "stick." The baculus was the name of the Grand Master's staff in the Knights Templar.

Bell: In Wicca, a small hand bell is often used during the casting and closing of a Circle and during rituals. The bell is used in many other magickal traditions as well. For example, in Voodoo, a small bell called a Clochette is held in the hand of the Houn'gan or Mambo along with the Asson (a sacred calabash rattle that is the symbol of their office) during ritual. An Ogan, a flattened iron bell without a clapper, played with an iron rod, is played in Voodoo rituals. In Santería, a small square silver bell called a Cencerro is used to summon the Orisha Obatala. A hand bell called an Agogo is used together with drums to invoke Orishas in Santería. A conical bell called an Irofa is used in Santería and Yoruban religion as one of the symbols of the Orisha Orunmila.

Beltaine: The Greater Sabbat that signalled the beginning of summer for the Celtic people was Beltaine. It occurs with the setting of the constellation of the Pleiades on April 30. Beltaine (literally "fires of Bel") was named for the solar deity known in various parts of the Celtic world as Beli, Bile, Belenos, Bel, and Belenus. Beltaine is known in Wales as Galan Mai. It is the other great fire festival, the first being Samhain. This is when the Celts drove their cattle to summer pasture.

Beltaine is an ancient celebration of fertility and life. At our celebrations we crown a young girl as "May Queen," representing the Maiden Goddess as well as a young man as "May King." Beltaine is another fire festival, but unlike Samhain, when the fires are lit at dusk, the Beltaine fires are lit at dawn. Traditionally, horns are sounded during the lighting of the fires.

Dancing around the Maypole is a Beltaine custom which continues in the British Isles to this day. The Maypole is an ancient fertility symbol. The British Maypole was a young tree that was chopped down on May Day and trimmed of all but a few branches at the top. It was then decorated and raised on the village green. In later years many towns had permanent poles. In 1644, Maypoles were forbidden throughout England and Wales by Cromwell's government. Many of the permanent poles came down. When King Charles II was restored to office on May 29, 1660, this prohibition was lifted and some of the Maypoles returned. Folklorist Christina Hole notes that, "The shorter poles, round which the children perform a plaited ribbon dance, and which are often seen at school May Day celebrations today, do not belong to the English tradition. They come from southern Europe, and seem to have been introduced into [England] (by Ruskin) in 1888."[6]

May Garlands are an ancient Beltaine custom. Many traditional May Day celebrations involve the carrying about of garlands. For this reason another name for Beltaine is "Garland Day." Children used to go from door to door with their garlands singing songs and receiving small gifts or coins. Often the garlands were in the form of a hoop, and in some places games evolved where a ball was thrown through or over the hoop. Sometime they took the form of floral globes, often with a May Doll suspended inside. In Horncastle in Lincolnshire, young boys carried peeled willow Wands covered with cowslips called "May Gads," which they carried in procession on May morning to the site of an old Roman temple where the Maypole stood. There they would strike them together to scatter the blossoms in honor of the first day of summer.

Another related custom was the dressing of wells and springs, in keeping with the Celtic customs of venerating such springs as connections to the Otherworld. At the Beltaine celebrations that we have participated in for the last decade, materials are laid out for people to use to decorate the well on the property.

Another Beltaine custom is the collection of dew. "May first is the magical time of greatest power for the element of water and 'wild' water (dew, flowing streams, or ocean water) is collected for the base of healing drinks and potions for the year to come."[7] Young girls would go out before dawn on May Day to collect dew and wash their faces with it. This was supposed to bring beauty and luck to them. It was also collected and kept to treat consumption, goiter, and various other ills.

"Hobby Horses" also make their appearance at Beltaine. This is similar to the custom of Hodening that occurs at Samhain and Yule. The most usual form is a hoop frame, six feet in diameter, covered with cloth skirting. In front is a wooden horse's head, with jaws that snap. A man stands inside, his head hidden by a mask. The Hobby Horse goes about with a group of attendants, the most important of which is often a "Teaser" or "Club Man" who carries a padded club and wears grotesque clothing. As they process down the streets the Hobby Horse will rush at girls and try to trap them under his skirts. This is thought to bring them fertility and/or a husband. The inside of the skirts was formerly smeared with blacking to leave a mark on the girl of her good fortune, but this is not done in modern survivals of this custom. Another discontinued custom was the sprinkling of water on the onlookers by the Hobby Horse when it stopped at a pool to "drink." Every so often the horse sinks down as if dying and the songs change from happy ones to sadder ones. The Teaser gently strokes him with his club. But after this brief pause the Hobby horse leaps up, the music returns to happier tunes and the procession continues.

Besom: This word comes from the Old English *besema* or *besma* (circa 800 C.E.), meaning a "bundle of twigs" that was used as a broom or as a flail. The Old Frisian word for a broom is also *besma*. The modern Dutch word for broom is *bezem*. The Witch's broom, used in Wiccan rituals, such as handfasting.

Blessed Be: The traditional words of welcome, blessing, and farewell used by Wiccans.

Bolline: A sickle or knife used for cutting herbs, engraving, etc., in Occidental Ceremonial Magick and in Wiccan ritual. Often has a white handle. The term "bolline" first appeared in the *Greater Key of Solomon* in reference to a tool of this sort. Another term for this knife used in Welsh traditions is Kerfan. Traditionally it is only used for ritual purposes and often is not used outside of a consecrated Circle.

Bonfire: The word "bonfire" comes originally from the Middle English term *balefyre,* from the Anglo Saxon *baelfyr.* Circa 1415 the word had become *banefire* and referred to fires into which the bones of cattle and sheep that had been saved during the year were burned. By 1552 the term was used to refer to fires on which corpses were burned. In 1556 it first appeared in its more modern spelling. By the end of the sixteenth century, the term was being used to refer to any large outdoor fire, the less common term *balefire* still being used in Wicca to refer to ritual fires.

Book of Shadows: In Wicca, a personal journal of rituals, rites, cures, and magick. The term was first used by the founder of modern Wicca, Gerald Gardner, who applied it to the journal of ritual and magick of his Coven. The original name of his journal was the *Book of Art Magical.* It seems that the reason that he chose this name and made references to the Inquisition in the Ordains that formed a part of it was to make it seem to be a survival from the burning times of the Inquisition, rather than his more recent collection of folklore. Surviving manuscripts and analysis of the language in Gardner's Book of Shadows prove that it cannot have been written during the Inquisition.

Some recent authors have begun to use the expression Book of Shadows as a synonym for Grimoire. While both a Grimoire and a Book of Shadows are magickal texts, they are different in several ways. A Book of Shadows documents Wiccan ritual and magick while a Grimoire is primarily a directory of Judaic and Christian spirits and Occidental Ceremonial magick. In Santería a similar handwritten journal, called a *Libreta,* is used.

Cauldron: Also known as a caldron. The Middle English word was *caldron* or *caudron,* and first appeared in Gower's Confessio Amantis before 1393. Before 1300 it was spelled *caudrun.* This word comes from the Old French *caudron* or *chaudron.* It derives from the late Latin *caldaria* ("a kettle for hot water").[8] A Cauldron is a large, iron pot, which is an ancient symbol of the Celtic Goddess Cerridwen or the Celtic God Dagda. To the Celts the Cauldron was an ancient symbol of rebirth and regeneration. Many ancient Celtic myths refer to the Cauldron as a sort of cornucopia which contains whatever food a person desires and is never empty. For example, the Dagda's Cauldron, named "the undry" or Uinde ("act of beholding") was never empty of food.

The Cauldron is the Greater Magickal Weapon of Water. Many Pagan and Neopagan religious groups use Cauldrons in their ritual Circles.

Chalice: A ceremonial cup or goblet often used to represent the element Water in magickal work. The Chalice is the Lesser Magickal Weapon of Water. The word Chalice first appeared in English about 1325. In Middle English (circa 1102) it was spelled *calice* and in Old English *celic, calic* or *caelc.* In old French it is *calix* ("cup") and it can be traced back through Greek (*kylix*) and Sanskrit (*kalasa-s*) to Indo-European (*kel/kol* = "pot, cup").[9]

The Chalice is used in the Wiccan ceremony of cakes and wine. Many other magickal traditions utilize the ritual Chalice, including the Knights Templar, Freemasons, and the Hermetic Order of the Golden Dawn.

Circle: The consecrated space within which a Wiccan ritual is held. In Occidental Ceremonial Magick, the circle is a defense, meant to keep unwanted influences and spirits *out.* A triangle is drawn on the ground outside of this ceremonial circle in whatever quarter is appropriate to the spirit being evoked or invoked. Most Grimoires describe one Circle which is used for all magickal operations, but there are exceptions. Honorius specified a general purpose circle as well as a different Circle for each day of the week. The Grand Grimoire specifies two circles—a Grand Kabalistic Circle and a Circle of White Magick.

In Neopagan religions such as Wicca, the Circle is a sacred space which may be created anywhere, as opposed to temples or churches in other religions, which are, of course, not portable. A Wiccan Circle is a container, meant to keep the energy that they raise *in* and unwanted influences *out.* It traditionally has a diameter of nine feet. This is a custom borrowed from the Greater Key of Solomon. The ritual Circle described in the Greater Key of Solomon is a triple circle: The inner circle has a radius of nine feet, with the second and third circles having a radius of ten and eleven feet respectively. In practice, the Circle is usually made larger, since a nine-foot Circle makes for a very small working area.

Wiccan circles may be "closed" or "open." Some Covens provide public rituals that are open to noninitiates. Such rituals are referred to as "Open Circles." Such public "Open Circles" are often referred to as "Pagan rituals" in order to differentiate them from "Closed Circles" or "Wiccan rituals" in which all of the participants are initiated Wiccans.

A Coven holding an Open Circle will usually use somewhat different ritual forms than they ordinarily use in Closed Circles, but this is not always the case. Examples of situations where one would find an open Circle are:

◆ Major public Pagan festivals, sponsored by various Wiccan and Pagan organizations. A few examples of such festivals are Dragonfest (Colorado), Spring Mysteries and Hecate's Sickle (Washington), Heartland (Kansas), Pagan Spirit Gathering or "PSG" (Ohio), and Gathering of the Tribes (Virginia). These have proved to be very popular, some of then attracting hundreds of participants. Open Circles are usually held at such festivals so that people from a variety of traditions and beliefs can come together and share ideas.

◆ An Open Circle where a candidate for initiation is allowed to participate in order to see if they can work harmoniously with the other Coven members.

◆ An Open Circle where a visitor is permitted to participate in the Circle of a Coven from a different tradition.

Coven: This word dates back to 1500–20 C.E. and was a variation of the earlier words *Covent* or *cuvent,* which are found in the Ancrene Riwle. It came into the English language through the Old French words *Covenant* and *Covenir.* These words came, in turn, from the Latin *convenire* ("to agree, to be of one mind, to come together"). Thus a Coven is a group of people who are of one mind, who come together with a common purpose.

   Coven first appeared in reference to "a gathering of witches" in 1662.[10] The word "Coven" is usually used today to refer to a Wiccan group, though it is sometimes used by the popular press to describe groups of Satanists, probably due to popular Christian literature. Modern Satanists actually refer to their groups as "Grottos" or "Pylons."

Covendom: In Wicca, the area around a Covenstead, three miles in diameter.

Covenstead: The regular meeting place of a Coven.

Cowan: The etymology of this word is uncertain, but it appears to be a term derived from the Greek word *kyon* ("a dog"). The use of this word in English originated in Scotland, where it was a term to describe a stone mason who has picked up his trade without serving an apprenticeship or to a mason who built "drystane dykes" (i.e., walls without mortar). Like a dog these persons were supposed to be inquisitive, sticking their noses into that which did not concern them.

   Cowan was adopted by the Freemasons from the Scottish stone masons to describe those who practice Freemasonry without having been properly initiated or to a person who is not of the brotherhood of Freemasonry. First appeared in this context in Anderson's *Constitutions* in 1769 C.E.[11]

   Wiccans borrowed this term from Freemasonry. Wiccans use it nowadays to describe someone who is not a Wiccan. Cowan may have been synonymous with "Warlock" (oath breaker) at one point, but is now generally a benign term for an outsider or noninitiate.

Craft, The: An expression used by Freemasons to describe their practices and beliefs. Gerald Gardner borrowed this term from them to describe their practices and beliefs of Wiccans.

Cross-Quarter Days: The "Greater" Celtic or Wiccan Sabbats, which fall between the Solstices and Equinoxes, including Samhain, Imbolc, Beltaine, and Lughnasad.

Deiseal: (Variations: *Deiseil, Deosil*) A Gaelic word meaning "toward the south" or "sunward course." It refers to clockwise or "sunwise" movement within a ritual Circle in Wiccan and Druid ceremonies. Usually spelled "deosil" in modern Wicca.

Eostre: Eostre (also known as Ostara or Alban Eiler) is the Lesser Sabbat that marks the Spring Equinox on March 21. Eostre marks the beginning of Spring in the modern world. It is a celebration of the return of life to the earth after the long winter. Its name derives from the Anglo-Saxon Goddess Eostre (or Ostara) was believed to fly over the earth, leaving the eggs (beginnings) of new life. Her totem animal was the rabbit.

 It is from this Sabbat and the name of this Germanic Goddess that the Christian festival of Easter was derived. In Old High German its name was *Ostarun,* becoming *Ostern* in Modern German. In Bede's *Ecclesiastical History* it was spelled *Eastre,* as it was in Old English before 899. By 1103 it had become *Estran.* In Middle English (before 1387), it was spelled *Ester* or *Esterne.*

Equinox: The word "equinox" can be traced back to the Latin term *aequinoctium,* which was derived from the terms *aequus* ("equal") and *nox* ("night").

 The Equinox is the time that the path of the sun crosses the equator, the time of year when the day and night are of equal length. The Spring, or Vernal, Equinox is around March 21 each year and the Fall, or Autumnal, Equinox is around September 21.

The Equinoxes are Lesser Sabbats in the Wiccan festival. The Spring Equinox is known as Eostre and the Autumnal Equinox is known as Mabon.

Esbat: It was the Egyptologist Margaret Murray who first used the term "Esbats" to describe mundane gatherings of witches. She obtained it from the Old French term *Esbatment,* which means "to divert oneself" or "an amusement."

Today Wiccans use the term "Esbat" to describe a ceremony occurring during a full moon. These are regular meetings where Wiccans celebrate rituals, discuss business, perform tasks such as healing, and enjoy each others' company. Occasionally Wiccans may also meet during the new moon in "Dark Moon" ceremonies and even during the first quarter (called "Diana's Bow") or the last quarter (called "Hecate's Sickle"), depending on what kind of work they wish to accomplish. For example, the period of the waning moon is considered by Wiccans to be a good time to work on banishing negative influences from your life.

Handfasting: This archaic word for marriage is now a modern term for a Wiccan or Neopagan wedding. It is derived from the Middle English term *handfasten* or *handfesten* (circa 1200 C.E.). There is a similar Icelandic word, *handfesta.* From *hond* ("hand") and *festa* ("to fasten" or "pledge").

Imbolc: Imbolc (also known as Imbolg, Uimelc, Oimelc, Feile Bhride, Brigid, Brigantia, or Candlemas) is the Greater Sabbat occurring on February 2. Imbolc is a celebration of the first signs of returning life in Spring. It was named by some as Oimelc ("Sheep's Milk") as it marked the beginning of the lambing season. It was celebrated by the Celts as being sacred to

Brigid (Bride, Brigit), a Celtic Goddess whose threefold aspect rules smith craft, poetry, inspiration, and healing (and who was later inducted as a Catholic saint). Hence one of the other names for this day is "Feile Bhride," meaning "Brigid's Feast." *Februum,* from which we derive the word for February, is a Latin word meaning "purification" and "atonement," thus this month is considered a month of cleansing. Many will recognize this date as being the current Groundhog Day. This dates back to the original festival when people sought out signs of the approaching Spring.

Initiate: A new member of a Coven, i.e., a Wiccan holding the rank of the first degree.

Litha: The Lesser Sabbat which follows Beltaine is Litha, which coincides with the Summer Solstice, the longest day of the year, June 21. Litha is a Saxon celebration incorporated into the Wiccan calendar as a celebration of the first fruits of the season. In some traditions, this day is celebrated as the Sacred Marriage of the Goddess and God. In others it is celebrated as the victory of the Lord of the Waning Year over the Lord of the Waxing Year, to mark the point from which the days will shorten.

Lughnasad: The Greater Sabbat that marks the first harvest is Lughnasad, which occurs on August 1. This festival is one of the Celtic fire festivals, or cross-quarter days. It is named in honor of the Celtic Sun God Lugh. Races and games are held in his name and that of Lugh's mother, Tailltiu.

Another name for this day is Lammas: This is the Saxon Feast of Bread, at which the first grain harvest is consumed in the form of ritual loaves. The name "Lammas" comes from the original Anglo Saxon name, *Hloaf Maesse* ("loaf mass" or "loaf feast"). A variation of this ritual that I have participated in for many years is the ritual drama of John Barleycorn, the life of the fields. John Barleycorn represents the grain that is cut down but returns to life again the following year.

Lustral Bath: This expression comes from the Middle French word *lustral* (circa 1533 C.E.), which derives from the Latin *lustrare,* which means "to spread light over" or "to brighten."[12] A bath of purification taken prior to a Wiccan ritual, usually consisting of consecrated water with a little salt. This is a custom borrowed from chapter 5 of book two of the *Greater Key of Solomon.*

Mabon: The Lesser Sabbat that follows Lughnasad is Mabon, which coincides with the Autumnal Equinox, occurring around September 21. Mabon is the second harvest festival. It is named for the Celtic Deity Mabon, son of Modron, who is mentioned in the story of Culhwch and Olwen. His name translates simply as "son." It is a time of thanksgiving for the bounty of the earth which will sustain us through the Winter. In the modern world it is the beginning of Autumn.

Magickal Weapons: Magickal Weapons are an element that Gardner borrowed from Ceremonial Magick when he laid down the basic structure of Wiccan ritual practice. In Ceremonial Magick they are often referred to as "Elemental Weapons."[13] For the Wiccan Warrior, there are several sets of Magickal Weapons that have been adopted from Celtic mythology. Steve Blamires grouped these Weapons into four double groups in his book *Glamoury.*[14] I have modified his groupings in my practice; I have identified five double groupings. This is because Blamires did not include Spirit as one of the elements in his list.

In my system, each group of Magickal Weapons is associated with an element. For Air (east): the dagger (Athame) or Sword. For Fire (south): the Wand or Spear. For Water (west): the Chalice or Cauldron. For Earth (north): the Pentacle (see glossary), Shield or Stone. The Magickal Weapon of Spirit is the Warrior's mind. Note that I spell the word "Weapon" beginning with a capital W in this work when I am using the word in reference to a Magickal Weapon.

These Magickal Weapons can be grouped into two categories, Greater and Lesser, as follows:

Greater Magickal Weapons

◆ Spirit

◆ Sword

◆ Spear

◆ Cauldron

◆ Shield

Lesser Magickal Weapons

◆ Mind

◆ Athame (dagger)

◆ Wand

◆ Chalice

◆ Pentacle or Stone

Neopagan: A Latin term meaning "New Pagan." Neopaganism can be defined as: "A group of modern Earth Religions which borrow and adapt concepts from pre-Christian Pagan Religions, often with additions from its own contemporary theologians."[15] (See *Pagan*).

Old Religion, the: This was a term originally coined by Margaret Murray in her books on Pagan religion in the 1920s. Murray was using it to describe the "Witch Cult of Western Europe" that she believed to be widespread in Europe around the time of the Inquisition. Modern scholars have proved that there was no such cult per se, but followers of the modern religion of Wicca and related Neopagan religions adopted this expression to describe their religions.

Pagan: This word first appeared in its modern spelling in 1425 in Higden's *Polychronicon.* In Mallory's *Morte D'Arthur* (circa 1400) it was spelled *paygan.* It can be traced back to the Latin root *pagus,* which originally meant "something stuck in the ground as a landmark." In other words, a "peg." *Pagus* was derived from the root *pag,* meaning "fix." A whole family of English words can be traced back to this same root, including the words "page" and "pole." The noun *paganus,* meaning "country dweller," was ultimately derived from the Latin term *pagus.*[16]

John Ayto theorizes that because early Christians considered themselves "soldiers" of Christ and because "paganus" later came to be used to refer to "civilians," the Christians adopted it to refer to non-Christians. Others have speculated that "paganus" was used by the predominantly city-dwelling early Christians to refer to non-Christians in much the same way as we would call someone a "hick" or "country bumpkin" today. We may never know for sure which of these theories is correct, but the fact remains that "pagan" ultimately became a term used by Christians to refer to non-Christians.

In recent years followers of many earth-based tribal religions have come to refer to their beliefs as "Pagan" or "Neopagan" ("New Pagan").

Paganing: See *Wiccaning.*

Pentacle: A pentagram within a circle. The Pentacle is the Lesser Magickal Weapon of Earth. In Wicca this usually takes the form of a flat, round disk with a pentagram in a circle engraved on it, representing the element of Earth. It is used to distribute cakes in a ritual (also spelled "pantacle" in this usage). It is traditionally made of wood, although I have seen metal, ceramic, and glass Pentacles/pantacles as well.

In some magickal traditions the Pentacle is a circular talisman with designs on it associated to its magickal purpose. Originally this referred to a five-pointed star (pentagram) on such a talisman, but in later use it was used to refer to talismans with other symbols such as the hexagram as well.

Pentagram: The Pentagram that is the symbol of Wicca is a five-pointed star formed by five straight lines, with one point uppermost, enclosed within a circle. As the pentagram consists of a continuous line that runs from point to point, it has been referred to as an "endless knot." It has taken thousands of years for the pentagram to evolve into this modern symbol. The pentagram is a very old symbol that has gradually gathered meaning unto itself over the centuries.

Pythagoras referred to the pentagram as the "pentalpha," since it represents the letter alpha (the letter *A*) in five different positions. The ancient Greeks used it as a talisman and preservative from danger, being inscribed on the threshold of a doorway. The Babylonians inscribed it on pots as a preservative amulet.[17] There is an ancient belief that a spirit needs some sort of "gate" to gain access to you. The fact that a pentagram can be drawn in one unbroken line (i.e., leaving no unbroken lines or "gates") was one of the reasons that it was believed to afford protection against spirits. Five-pointed stars are found in ancient Egyptian, Greek, and Roman art, and also in that of the Christian early Middle Ages, but there seems to have been no single tradition concerning their meaning and use, and in many contexts they seem simply to have been decorative.[18]

It was in the twelfth century Renaissance period that Honorius of Autun and Hildegard of Bingen asserted that the human body was constructed upon the basis of the number five and related it to a pentagram. They pointed out that the human body had five members, five senses, and five figures.

This belief that the pentagram was a symbol of the microcosmos developed into a belief that it was a magickal symbol. William of Auvergne wrote that the pentagram was mentioned in the Liber Sacer, which was alleged to have been written by the philosopher magician "Honorius, Master of Thebes." Between the fourteenth and seventeenth centuries, three recensions describe the "seal of the living God" as a pentagram and two hexagrams surrounded by angelic names. These texts assert that this "seal" has power over spirits.[19] This is the source of the confusion surrounding both the pentagram and the hexagram being referred to in various texts and Grimoires as "Solomon's Seal."

A pentagram is the symbol that appears on the shield of Sir Gawaine in the fourteenth-century poem, *Sir Gawaine and the Green Knight*. It is in this poem that the author indicates that the pentagram is an "endless knot" and states that it represented the five wounds of Christ.

The pentagram next appears in the sixteenth century in Cornelius Agrippa's *De Occulta Philosophia*. In this book the magician is instructed to draw pentagrams at the cardinal points of the Magickal Circle to protect it.

Lazarus Meysonnier, a Hermetic philosopher living in Lyon, wrote a whole book describing the pentagram in 1659, his *Pentagonum Philosphico-Medicum*. Meysonnier wrote that the pentagram was a symbol of the firmament, the planets, and the elements.

In the middle of the seventeenth century, one of the fathers of modern Freemasonry, Sir Robert Moray, adopted the pentagram as a Masonic symbol of love and charity. By the nineteenth century the Freemasons had adopted the pentagram as a symbol of the most sacred principles.

It was also in the nineteenth century that Eliphas Levi reinforced the idea that the pentagram represented the microcosm of the universe. It was Levi who first introduced the idea that the pentagram could be used for invoking: Previous to this the pentagram was primarily associated with banishing negative influences.[20] Nowadays followers of many traditions of both Wicca and Ceremonial Magick trace the symbol of the pentagram in the air during rituals for both banishing and invoking. As a general rule, one commences by tracing toward the angle of the pentagram representing the element being invoked, and away from that angle while banishing.

The Hermetic Order of the Golden Dawn associated the pentagram with Mars and with the Hebrew letter *Heh.* The Golden Dawn called it the "Flaming Pentagram" or "the Star of the Great Light." Regardie, in his book *The Complete Golden Dawn System of Magic,* referred to the pentagram as the "Signet Star of the Microcosm," representing the operation of the Spirit and the four elements under the presidency of the Pentagrammaton (literally "five-letter word; i.e., the name YHShVH, also known as Yesheshuah, Yeheshuah, or Hehovashah).

Inverted, that is, with two points uppermost instead of one, the pentagram has been used as a symbol of several different things. Within some traditions of Wicca an inverted pentagram has been used as a symbol of the second degree of initiation. An inverted pentagram is a symbol of the Masonic women's organization, The Order of the Eastern Star. The highest decoration for valor in the U.S. is the Medal of Honor, which is an inverted pentagram. Aleister Crowley used the inverted pentagram to symbolize the descent of Spirit into matter.[21]

It was Eliphas Levi in the nineteenth century who started the idea that the inverted pentagram was a symbol of Satan.[22] Levi interpreted the four points of the elements over the point of spirit as representing the domination of Matter over Reason, which Levi believed to be a characteristic of Satanism. Coincidentally, an inverted pentagram also resembles a goat's head when inverted, though this is probably a very recent

interpretation. Others have presented alternative interpretations. Barbara G. Walker has reported that the inverted pentagram represents the Horned God.[23]

In the 1960s Anton LaVey capitalized on Levi's interpretation. LaVey used an inverted pentagram on a circular field
with a goat's head superimposed over it as a symbol of the
Church of Satan that he founded. LaVey referred to this logo
as the Sigil of Baphomet. Doubtless this was inspired by the
image of "The Sabbatic Goat" in Levi's book *Transcendental
Magic*.[24] The Temple of Set, a group which broke away from
LaVey's Church of Satan, has also adopted the inverted pentagram against a circular field as their official symbol.

The apple is considered a fruit sacred to the Goddess. If
you cut an apple in half across its axis, you will discover that
the core and seeds form a pentagram. This is one of the reasons that the pentagram is a sacred symbol for Wiccans.

Rede: Derived from the Anglo-Saxon word *raedan,* meaning "to
interpret." A rule governing interpretation. A term used in
Wicca for a religious law or maxim. The most important guid-
ing principle for Wiccans is the "Wiccan Rede," which is, "Do
whatever you will, so long as it does not harm another."

Sabbat/Sabbath: This term comes from the Hebrew term *Shabbath*
("rest"), which later became *Sabbaton* in Greek and *Sabbatum* in
Latin. It appeared as *Sabbat* in Old English circa 950 C.E.

Originally, in Judaism and in Christianity, the Sabbat was a
day of rest, being the seventh day after the creation of the
world, according to the Bible. In Judaism and some Christian
sects this is Saturday, but in most other Christian denominations it is Sunday.

The Wiccan use of the term "Sabbat" was derived from the
works of Margaret Murray. Murray used the term "Sabbats" to
refer to the major celebrations of Pagans persecuted as Witches
during the Inquisition. Murray borrowed it from the works of

early demonologists, who used the term to describe alleged meetings of Witches because the same demonologists held Judaism to be the antithesis of Christianity. Wiccans now use the term to describe the major Wiccan festivals, marking the turning of the seasons of the year. There are eight Sabbats evenly spaced throughout the year: Samhain, Yule, Imbolc, Eostre, Beltaine, Litha, Lughnasad, and Mabon.

Samhain: The Greater Sabbat that marks the beginning of the Wiccan year on October 31. It is also known in Wales as Calan Gaef or Nos Galan-Gaeof. Samhain marks the rising of the constellation of the Pleiades, which is to be found in the constellation Taurus. This celebration is the source of much of the modern folklore surrounding the modern holiday of Halloween. It was a time of truce, when councils are held, legal judgments passed, and agreements made.

Modern Wiccans celebrate Samhain as New Year's Eve, as the ancient Celts did. Being the turning of the year, this time between the years is considered a time at which the barriers between the worlds of life and death are as thin as veils. This is the time when the spirits of our ancestors can return, to be welcomed by their kin and celebrate with them. This is where much of the ghost folklore related to the modern holiday of Halloween originated. Wiccans view Samhain as a time to honor those who have gone before us, not to fear them.

Lighting candles in remembrance is an old Samhain custom. The flame in each of the punkies represents the spirits of the departed that are remembered on Samhain. All over Europe it was customary on Samhain to leave lighted candles in the windows to guide the spirits of departed relatives back to visit you.

In Ireland and Brittany, food and drink was set out for the spirits of the departed, often referred to as the "Dumb Supper." Soul cakes may have originally been the food that was offered. Modern Wiccans often observe Samhain by serving a feast called a "Dumb Supper" at which strict silence is observed. A place is set at the table for the spirits.

Samhain is a fire festival. Bonfires were lit all over Britain at Samhain. In many parts of Britain these fires were known as "Teanlas," "Teanlay," "Tindles," or "Tandles." Farmers would carry aloft pitch forks of flaming straw, burning splinters, or smoldering faggots from these fires and carry them around the fields to bless them. In Wales, people used to light bonfires on hilltops at Samhain. They would roast potatoes and apples to eat, dance and sing, and when the fire burned down, leap over it. Samhain is traditionally a time of divination. Divination is important to the Warrior as it helps her plan her path (see the Book of Water for a discussion of divination). This was a very important aspect of Samhain, since so many different forms of divination were traditionally practiced on this day. Here are some examples.

- It was customary in both Wales and Scotland to mark a white stone and either throw it into the fire or place it in a ring of stones around it. The next morning the person would return to search for the stone. If it was unharmed this was a good omen, but if it was cracked the omens for the coming year were bad.

- One form of divination involves peeling an apple in one long, continuous strip, then throwing the peel over your left shoulder at midnight. The initials of your future lover's name were supposed to be revealed by the form the peel took when it landed.

- Other forms of apple divination involved eating an apple in front of a mirror. The face of your future lover was supposed to appear behind your left shoulder.

- Another traditional method is to take two nuts, each representing one of a couple, and place them in the embers of the fire. If they burn away quietly, the two will marry, but if they explode or flare up, the courtship is fated to fail.

◆ In North Lancashire a ceremony of "Lating the Witches" takes place at Samhain, where people light candles and carry them over the hills between 11 P.M. and midnight. If the candle remained lit then the person that it had been lit for was safe for the coming year, but if it went out, misfortune might be expected.

◆ Another custom is the placing of twelve candles in a ring on the floor. People would jump the candles in turn, each candle representing a month of the year. If one went out when a person jumped over it, this meant that misfortune would befall that person in that month.

◆ In Scotland charms of various shapes were concealed in a bowl of mashed potatoes, which was then passed around. Each person would take a spoonful. The charm you find in your portion is an omen of the coming year. A coin would mean prosperity, a wishbone the achieving of a wish, and so on. This custom was also practiced in Wales, where the charms were concealed in a bowl of mashed vegetables.

An ancient custom still practiced in Ireland and Scotland is guising, the forerunner of the current "Trick or Treat" custom in North America. A procession of horn-blowing youths went from house to house fantastically dressed, collecting money or gifts of food. A related custom was "Hodening" or "Hoodening." A man would bear a horse's skull (or wooden horse's head) on a pole. The jaws of the horse's head were often wired and made to snap open and shut. Some of these horse skulls had candles inside them to cast an eerie light. The man bearing the skull covered himself with a stable blanket or sheet. This "Hooden Horse" would go from house to house accompanied by "soulers" who sang traditional seasonal songs.[25] The horse is a symbol of Celtic Goddesses like Epona and Rhiannon. Often the soulers were children, who would sing their ancient souling-songs from door to door in return for gifts or food. In some places special cakes called "Soul cakes," "Saumas cakes," "Soulmas cakes," "Dole cakes," or "Dirge loaves" were traditionally handed out to soulers.

The modern "Jack o' Lantern" has a long history. One of the colloquial names for Halloween in Sommerset is "Punkie Night." It got this name from the "punkies," or candle lanterns, which the children would make from hollowed-out gourds such as mangold-wurzels. In other places turnips or cabbage stalks (called in Scotland a *custock*) were used to make lanterns. The children did not necessarily carve faces into them. Punkies were often carved with elaborate designs of animals, flowers, etc.

Shield: The Greater Magickal Weapon of Earth. This word can be traced back to the Anglo Saxon terms *scild, scyld,* or *sceld,* which translated as "shield," "refuge," or "protection." The shield was originally a piece of protective armor carried in the hand or worn on the forearm. Nowadays the shield is often a heraldic device used as a symbol of a family or institution or as a plaque or trophy.

Skyclad: A colloquial English term for nudity. Ritual nudity is common in some Wiccan traditions.

Solstice: This word can be traced back to the Latin term *solstitium,* derived from the roots *sol* ("sun") and *statum* ("to stand still"). The solstice is the point in the sun's path (ecliptic) when it is at the greatest distance from the equator, being the time of year when the difference in length between day and night are at their greatest. The Summer Solstice is approximately June 21 each year and the Winter Solstice is approximately December 21. The Summer Solstice is sometimes known as the North Solstice, since it is the northernmost point that the sun reaches in its yearly cycle. Similarly the Winter Solstice is often known as the South Solstice, since this is the southernmost part of the sun's yearly cycle.

In Neopagan religions, such as Wicca, the Solstices are Lesser Sabbats. The Winter Solstice is called Yule and the Summer Solstice is called Litha.

Spear: The Spear is the Greater Magickal Weapon of Fire. In Wiccan practice is is usually represented by the Staff or Stang.

Staff: This is derived from the Anglo Saxon term *staef* meaning "stick." This was a shoulder-high stick used for support in walking or as a weapon. In many cultures it became a symbol of authority. In modern Wiccan practice the Staff is used to represent the Spear, a Greater Magickal Weapon (see *Spear*).

Stang: This is derived from an Anglo Saxon term, *staeng* or *steng*, which translates as "pole" or "rod." A traditional Wiccan stang is a staff, shoulder height in length, with a fork at the top resembling the horns or antlers of the male animal. In modern Wiccan practice, the Stang is used as a Greater Magickal Weapon of Fire instead of the Spear (see *Spear*).

Sunwise: see *Deosil.*

Sword: A ritual Sword is often used in casting the ritual Circles of several different magickal traditions. The Sword is the Greater Magickal Weapon of Air. Each Wiccan Coven usually has one. The Sword is listed as a magickal tool in most Grimoires of Occidental Ceremonial Magick, and is used by such groups as the Hermetic Order of the Golden Dawn.

Thurible: Derived the Latin *thuribulum* ("a censer"), which was in turn derived from *thuris,* the Latin name for frankincense, a substance which was commonly used in incense. An incense burner or brazier. Often used in ritual as a symbol of the element of Air.

Wand: This word originated in Middle English describes a slender rod or staff. Traditionally the length of the Wiccan Wand is one cubit, the distance from the finger tips to the elbow. It is sometimes called a Baculum (See *Baculum*). The Wand is the Lesser Magickal Weapon of Fire.

Wicca: The Old English word *wicce,* meaning a female sorcerer, dates back to about 1000 c.e. "Wicce" is a feminine version of the even older word *wicca,* originally pronounced "witcha," although most people pronounce it as it would be in common English usage these days. Wicca originally referred to a *male* sorcerer or wizard, and first appeared in Old English about 890 c.e. "Wicce" and "Wicca" probably both derive from the Old English *wiccian,* which means "to practice sorcery," and is related to the Old English words *Wigle* (divination) and *wiglian* ("to divine"). Similar words are found in Old Frisian (*Wigila,* which translates as "sorcery"), Middle Low German and Middle High German (*wicken,* "to bewitch," *weihen,* "to consecrate" and *wikken,* "to divine"). Recent studies indicate that "wicca" derives from the Sanskrit root word *wik* or *weik,* meaning "to shape" or "to bend or turn." Thus Wicca could be interpreted as "shaper or bender (of reality)."

Whatever its roots, a "Wicca" now generally used to identify a follower of the Wiccan faith—a Witch. In its modern usage, the word "Wicca" has no gender and can properly be used to describe both male and female. However, some modern Wiccans employ the original Old English usage: "Wicca" for a male and "Wicce" for a female follower. The words "Wicca," "Wicce," and "Wiccan" can each be used as a descriptive term for a Witch.

Wiccaning: This is a Wiccan custom in which the parents of a child present the child to the deities and take oaths promising to raise and nurture the child properly and responsibly, usually assisted by other Coven members. This is customarily done between an infant's third and thirteenth month, though the custom varies.

Widdershins: A term derived from the High German *Widersinnes* and Low German *weddersinnes,* meaning "opposite sense" or "contradiction." This word first appeared in the English language circa 1545, meaning "a direction contrary to the source of the sun." This was believed to be unlucky and the cause of disasters. By 1721 it was used to mean "the wrong direction."

Widdershins is a term used by modern Wiccans as a synonym for counterclockwise. It is used to describe the counterclockwise direction of travel used in the ritual circle for banishing rituals. It is symbolic of decrease and sometimes chaos.

Yule: Yule is the Lesser Sabbat that follows Samhain, coinciding with the Winter Solstice around December 21. The word "Yule" first appeared in its modern spelling in 1475 C.E. Circa 1450 C.E. it was spelled "Yoole" and circa 1200 C.E. it appeared in *The Ormulum* as "Yole." Before 899 C.E. it appeared in Old English as the word *Geol* or *Geola.* The venerable Bede recorded it circa 726 C.E. in his history (written in Anglian Old English) as *Giuli.* It may have originated in Scandinavian countries, since their word for this season is similar, *jul.* In old Icelandic it is *jol.*[26]

As a matter of interest, the term "Christmas" cannot be traced back as far as the term "Yule." It first appeared as *Cristmessa,* or "Christ's festival" around 1100 C.E. Another Old English variation was *Cristes Maesse.* The expression "Christmas Eve" did not appear before 1300 C.E. (from "Cristenmesse Even"), Christmastide appeared in 1626 and although decorated trees appeared in England in the mid 1700s, the term "Christmas Tree" did not appear until 1835.[27]

The Lesser Sabbat of Yule marks the Winter Solstice: the longest night of the year. It is a festival of light commemorating the Goddess as Mother giving birth (once again) to the Sun God. I get up before the sun rises, light a bonfire and greet the sunrise with song. Our Coven stands around the fire, "singing the sun up" in celebration of the returning light. I have also attended Yule celebrations in which a ritual drama is enacted to represent the Young Lord (or the waxing year) emerging victorious over the Old Lord (the waning year).

It is customary to light a large, decorated, red, green, or blue candle called the Yule Candle. We leave it burning all day. Traditionally it was considered a very bad omen if anything caused it to go out. A Yule candle should never be blown out, as this supposedly brings bad luck too. It should be snuffed out with tongs at the end of the day. The remainder of the candle is kept until next Yule for good luck.

A variation of this is the lighting of the Yule Log. This is brought in at dusk and lit from a fragment of last year's log. The variation I practice is lighting the Yule sunrise bonfire with a fragment of last year's log. It is considered very unlucky to buy one. You should fetch your own, although it is perfectly acceptable to receive one as a gift. Yule Logs are often decorated before being brought in and consecrated by having offerings of wine and grain poured over it. Like the Yule Candle, the Yule Log is left alight all day. It is never allowed to burn entirely away. Like the Yule Candle, it must never go out until it is deliberately quenched. What remains is saved until next year, to light the next Yule Log and to bring good luck throughout the year.

After the Yule feast, some Wiccans go "Wassailing." This word comes from the Anglo Saxon words *wes* ("be thou") and *hal* ("whole"). Participants pass around a wassail bowl with some sort of hot drink in it. One of the most common traditional drinks was "Lamb's Wool," a mixture of hot ale, spices, sugar, and roasted apples, to which eggs and thick cream were sometimes added. The bowl was passed around for all to partake or, if it was too large for this, individual cups would be filled from it. A variation on this was for wassailers to go from door to door bearing their wassail bowl and singing traditional songs.

Farm workers would go about their property, toasting the trees, especially fruit trees, with strong ale or cider (which, being made of apples, was sacred to the Goddess). Some of the drink would be poured out on the roots or in the fork of the branches and branches would be pulled down and dipped in the drink. Offerings of bread or cakes were left in the tree for its spirit. In some areas the men showed the tree what was expected of it by miming the actions of picking up heavy bushels of apples. Livestock would be wassailed too.

Another old custom that I have practiced over the years is "First Foot." The first visitor to enter a house on Yule morning is known as the "First Foot." The First Foot should be a person from outside the home if possible. The First Foot brings in the luck of the New Year. The First Foot arrives bearing small gifts, usually including a piece of bread, a sprig of evergreen, a piece of coal, and a coin, symbolizing food, warmth, and wealth in the coming year. The First Foot bears these through every room in the house.

Endnotes

1. Grillot de Givry. (1954). *Witchcraft, Magic and Alchemy*, pp. 102–103.

2. Ibid., pp. 90, 133.

3. Arthur E. Waite. (1973). *The Book of Black Magic and Ceremonial Magic*, p. 154.

4. Doreen Valiente. (1978). *Witchcraft for Tomorrow*, p. 78.

5. Barbara Walker. (1988). *The Women's Dictionary of Symbols and Sacred Objects*, p. 21.

6. Christina Hole. (1976). *British Folk Customs*, p. 137.

7. (1990). "Wicca and Paganism: A Rebirth of the Religion of the Mother Goddess," *The Center for Non-Traditional Religion*, p. 9.

8. Robert K. Barnhart, ed. (1988). *Barnhart Dictionary of Etymology*, p. 135.

9. Ibid., p. 157.

10. Ibid., p. 228.

11. Anderson. *Constitutions*, p. 97.

12. Robert K. Barnhart, ed. (1988). *Barnhart Dictionary of Etymology*, p. 613.

13. Dion Fortune. (1978). *Moon Magic,* p. 80.

14. Steve Blamires. (1995). *Glamoury: Magic of the Celtic Green World,* p. 292.

15. Ed Fitch. (1988). *Magickal Rites from the Crystal Well,* p. 5

16. Robert K. Barnhart, ed. (1988). *Barnhart Dictionary of Etymology,* p. 746. John Ayto. (1990). *Dictionary of Word Origins,* p. 379.

17. Barbara G. Walker. (1983). *The Woman's Encyclopedia of Myths and Secrets,* p. 782.

18. Ronald Hutton. (1999). *Triumph of the Moon,* p. 67.

19. Ibid., p. 68.

20. Eliphas Levi. (1896, fourth impression 1974). *Transcendental Magic,* pp. 63-70.

21. Ronald Hutton. (1999). *Triumph of the Moon,* p. 179.

22. Eliphas Levi. (1896, fourth impression 1974). *Transcendental Magic,* pp. 63–70.

23. Barbara G. Walker. (1983). *The Woman's Encyclopedia of Myths and Secrets,* p. 783.

24. Elipas Levi. (1896, fourth impression 1974). *Transcendental Magic,* p. 186.

25. Christina Hole. (1976). *British Folk Customs,* pp. 100–102.

26. Robert K. Barnhart, ed. (1988). *Barnhart Dictionary of Etymology,* p. 1255.

27. Ibid., p. 170.

A Call for Rituals

IF YOU HAVE exeperienced a particularly powerful or significant ritual in your life and would like to share it with others, please drop me a line. Phoenix McFarland and I are collecting rituals to be included in an upcoming work on rituals.

You can contact me at:

kcuhulain@aol.com

Bibliography

Amiel, Henri-Frédéric. (1885). *Journal Intime.* MacMillan and Co., New York, N.Y.

Ayto, John. (1990). *Dictionary of Word Origins.* Arcade Publishing, New York, N.Y.

Bachelard, Gaston. (1971). *The Poetics of Reverie.* Beacon Press, Boston, Mass.

Bacon, Francis. (1900). *The Advancement of Learning.* Colonial Press, New York, N.Y.

Barney, Natalie Clifford. (1962). Quoted in "Gods," in *Adam.* N. 299 (London, 1962).

Barnhart, Robert K. ed. (1988). *Barnhart Dictionary of Etymology.* H.W. Wilson Co., New York, N.Y.

Barrie, J. M. (3 May 1922). Rectorial address at St. Andrew's University, Scotland.

Bear, Sun. (1985). Presentation in California.

Beckett, Samuel (1983). *Worstward Ho.* Grove Press, New York, N.Y.

Beckwith, Carol and Angela Fisher. (Sep 1999). "Masai Passage to Manhood," *National Geographic* magazine, Vol. 196, No. 3.

Bergson, Henri. (1988). *Matter and Memory.* Zone Books, New York, N.Y.

Bergson, Henri, and Mabelle Andison (tr.). (1968). *The Creative Mind.* Greenwood Press, New York, N.Y.

Bernanos, Georges. (1968). *The Last Essays of Georges Bernanos.* Greenwood Press, New York, N.Y.

Bierce, Ambrose. (1993). *The Devil's Dictionary.* Dover Publications, New York, N.Y.

Blacking, John. (1973). *How Musical Is Man?* University of Washington Press, Seattle, Wash.

Blamires, Steve. (1995). *Glamoury: Magic of the Celtic Green World.* Llewellyn Publications, St. Paul, Minn.

Bolitho, William. (1930). *Twelve Against the Gods.* the Press of the Reader's Club, New York, N.Y.

Bradley, F. H. (1951). *Appearance and Reality: A Metaphysical Essay.* Clarendon Press, Oxford.

Brookner, Anita. (1988). *Writers at Work.* (Eighth series, edited by George Plimpton, 1988), Penguin USA, New York, N.Y.

Brown, Norman O. (1990). *Love's Body.* University of California Press, Berkeley, Calif.

Carlyle, Thomas. (1833–34). *Sartor Resartus.* A.L. Burt Co., New York, N.Y.

Cary, Joyce. (1957). Interview in *Writers at Work* (First Series, ed. by Malcolm Cowley, 1958), Penguin USA, New York, N.Y.

Casteneda, Carlos. (1974). *Journey to Ixtlan.* Pocket Books, New York, N.Y.

———. (1974). *Tales of Power.* Simon & Schuster, Markham, Ontario.

Center for Non-Traditional Religion. (1990). "Wicca and Paganism: A Rebirth of the Religion of the Mother Goddess," The Center for Non-Traditional Religion, p. 9.

Cooley, Charles Horton. (1956). *Human Nature and the Social Order.* Free Press, Glencoe, Ill.

Crowley, Aleister. *Magick in Theory and Practice.* Castle Books, New York, N.Y., Introduction.

cummings, e.e. (1951). "Jotting," *Wake.* N. 10.

Cunningham, Scott. (1989). *Wicca: A Guide for the Solitary Practitioner.* Llewellyn Publications, St. Paul, Minn.

Curott, Phyllis. (2000). "Exploding Wiccan Dogma," lecture at Blessed Be and Merry Meet in DC (BBMMDC) conference in Washington D.C., 14 October 2000.

Davies, Robertson. (1985). *What's Bred in the Bone.* Blackstone Audio Books. N.p.

De Givry, Grillot. (1954). *Witchcraft, Magic and Alchemy.* Frederick Publications. N.p.

De Laurence, L. W., ed. (1914). *The Greater Key of Solomon.* Health Research, Mokelumne Hill, Calif.

Dhammananada, K. Sri. (1987). *Meditation: The Only Way.* Buddhist Missionary Society, Kuala Lumpur.

Doyle, Sir Arthur Conan. (1892). "The Speckled Band" from *Sherlock Holmes: The Complete Novels and Stories* (Bantam edition, 1986). Bantam Books, New York, N.Y.

Dylan, Bob. (1985). Interview in booklet accompanying the *Biograph* album set.

Elliot, George. (1999). *Middlemarch.* Oxford University Press, Toronto, Ontario.

Emerson, Ralph Waldo. (1971). *Works.* Belknap Press, Cambridge, Mass.

Farrar, Stewart. (1971). *What Witches Do: The Modern Coven Revealed.* Coward, McCann & Geoghegan, Inc., New York, N.Y.

Farrar, Janet, and Stewart Farrar. (1984). *A Witches Bible, Volume II: The Rituals.* Magickal Childe, New York, N.Y.

Fitch, Ed. (1988). *Magickal Rites from the Crystal Well.* Llewellyn Publications, St. Paul, Minn.

Fitzgerald, Penelope. (1990). *The Gate of Angels.* Collins, London.

Fortune, Dion. (1978). *Moon Magic.* Samuel Weiser, York Beach, Maine.

Frank, Philipp. (1950). *Einstein: His Life and Times.* Beacon Press, Boston, Mass.

Franklin, Benjamin. (1923). *Autobiography.* Houghton Mifflin Co., New York, N.Y.

Gibran, Kahil. (1962). *A Second Treasury of Kahil Gibran.* Citadel Press, New York, N.Y.

Haldane, J. B. S. (1932). "God-Makers," from *The Inequality of Man and Other Essays.* Chatto & Windus, London.

Harrow, Judy. "Basics for Beginners," Protean Book of Shadows, Proteus Coven, 1993.

Hart, Mickey. (1990). *Drumming at the Edge of Magic.* Harper San Francisco, San Francisco, Calif.

Havel, Václav. (1990). *Disturbing the Peace.* Knopf, New York, N.Y.

Hawthorne, Nathaniel. (1991). *The Blithedale Romance.* Oxford University Press, Oxford.

Heinlein, Robert A. (1987). *Stranger in a Strange Land.* Ace Books, New York, N.Y.

Heraclitus (Guy Davenport, trans.). (1976). *Herakleitos & Diogenes.* Grey Fox Press, Bolinas, Calif.

Herbert, George. (1651). *Jacula Prudentum.* Printed by T. Maxey for T. Garthwait, London.

Hole, Christina. (1976). *British Folk Customs.* Hutchinson & Co., London.

Hutton, Ronald. (1999). *Triumph of the Moon.* Oxford University Press, Oxford.

Huxley, Thomas Henry. (1925). *Collected Essays.* MacMillan, New York, N.Y.

Keats, John. (1951). *Selections.* Modern Library, New York, N.Y.

Johnson, Samuel. (1929). *The History of Rasselas.* Clarendon Press, Oxford.

Kragburn, Francine, ed. (1972). "The First Ms. Reader," *Columbia Dictionary of Quotations.* New York, N.Y.

K, Amber. (1990). *True Magick: A Beginner's Guide.* Llewellyn Publications, St. Paul, Minn.

La Rochefoucauld, François. (1959). *Sentences et Maximes Morales.* Random House, New York, N.Y.

Kit, Wong Kiew. (1997). *Chi Kung: For Health and Vitality.* Element Books, Shaftesbury, Dorset.

Lee, Bruce. (1975). *Tao of Jeet Kune Do.* Ohara Publications, Inc., Santa Clarita, Calif.

Le Guin, Ursula K. (Aug. 1990). "Winged: the Creatures on my Mind," in *Harper's* magazine, New York, N.Y.

Levi, Eliphas. (1896; fourth impression, 1974). *Transcendental Magic*. Samuel Weiser, Inc., New York, N.Y.

Lichtenberg, G. C. (1765–99). "Notebook F," from *Aphorisms* (trans. by R. J. Hollingdale, 1990).

Longfellow, Henry Wadsworth. (1839). "The Story of Brother Berdardus," in *Hyperion*. Houghton Mifflin, Boston, Mass.

Luc Vauvenargues, Marquis de. (1746). *Refléxions et Maximes*. Roger Charbonnel, Paris, Croville.

Madden, Kristin. (2000). *Pagan Parenting: Spiritual, Magical and Emotional Development of the Child*. Llewellyn Publications, St. Paul, Minn.

Mayne, Jonathan. (1965). *The Mirror of Art*. Phaidon Publishing, London.

McFarland, Phoenix. (1996). *The Complete Book of Magical Names*. Llewellyn Publications, St. Paul, Minn.

———. (1994). Position Paper, "A Few Controversial Thoughts on Drawing Down the Moon."

Millman, Dan. (1980). *The Way of the Peaceful Warrior*. H. J. Kramer, Tiburton, Calif.

Mitchell, Dr. Edgar, and Dwight Williams. (1996). *The Way of the Explorer*. G. P. Putnam's Sons, New York, N.Y.

Moore, Robert, and Douglas Gillette. (1992). *The Warrior Within: Accessing the Knight in the Male Psyche*. HarperCollins, San Francisco, Calif.

———. (1990). *King, Warrior, Magician, Lover: Rediscovering the Archetypes of the Mature Masculine*. Harper San Francisco, San Francisco, Calif.

Musashi, Miyamoto. (1988). "Introduction," *The Book of Five Rings*. Bantam Books, New York, N.Y.

Nelson, Portia. (1977). *There's a Hole in My Sidewalk.* Beyond Words Publishing, Hillsboro, Ore.

Noonan, Peggy (1990). *What I Saw at the Revolution.* Random House, New York, N.Y.

O'Gaea, Ashleen, and Carol Garr. (2000). *Circles Behind Bars: A Complete Handbook for the Incarcerated Witch.* Unpublished.

O'Rourke, P. J. (30 Nov 1989). *Rolling Stone* magazine.

Pound, Ezra. (1885–1972). "Ancient Music," from *Bartlett's Familiar Quotations,* sixteenth edition (1992). Little, Brown & Co., Boston, Mass.

Pound, Omar, and A. Walton Litz, eds. (1985). *Ezra Pound and Dorothy Shakespear: Their Letters 1909–1914.* New Directions, New York, N.Y.

Price, Brian R. (April 1997). "A Code of Chivalry: Modern, based on the 'Old Code.'" Website: www.chronique.com/Library/Chivalry?code.htm.

Rabelais, François. (1940). *Gargantua and Pantagruel.* Houghton, Boston, Mass.

RavenWolf, Silver. (2000). *Teen Witch: Wicca for a New Generation.* Llewellyn Publications, St. Paul, Minn.

Reich-Ranicki, Marcel. (1987; trans. from German by Ralph Manheim, 1989). *Thomas Mann and His Family.* Collins, London.

Rosenberg, Harold. (1960). *The Tradition of the New.* Horizon Press, New York, N.Y.

Schreiner, Olive. (1883). *The Story of an African Farm.* Modern Library, New York, N.Y.

Shakespeare, William (Stanley Wells and Gary Taylor, eds). (1988). *William Shakespeare: The Complete Works.* Clarendon Press, Oxford.

Shaw, George Bernard. (1856–1950). "Maxims for Revolutionists: Liberty and Equality," from *Man and Superman*. Chelsea House, New York, N.Y.

Shelley, Percy Bysshe. (1816). "Hymn to Intellectual Beauty," from the *Norton Anthology of English Literature*, Major Authors edition (Abrams, ed., 1940). W.W. Norton, New York, N.Y.

Shepherd, Cybill, and Paula Yoo. (29 June 1998). "Meno-Peace: A Star Discovers That the Change of Life Need Not Be One for the Worse," *People* magazine, Volume 49, No. 25.

Slater, Kate. (1994). Position Paper on Drawing Down, "Hearing Voices."

Stanley, Thomas J. Ph.D., and William D. Danko, Ph.D. (1996). *The Millionaire Next Door*. Pocket Books, New York, N.Y.

Steinem, Gloria. (1978). "Far From the Opposite Shore," in *Ms.* (New York, July 1978 and July/Aug. 1982; repr. 1983 in *Outrageous Acts and Everyday Rebellions*. H. Holt, New York, N.Y.)

Stevens, Wallace. (1951; first published 1947). "The Necessary Angel," from the *Columbia Dictionary of Quotations*. Columbia University Press, New York, N.Y.

Stewart, R. J. (1990). *Celtic Gods, Celtic Goddesses*. Blandford, London.

Sun Tzu (Thomas Cleary, trans.). (1991). *The Art of War*. Shambhala, Boston, Mass.

Thompson, Francis (Wilfrid Meynell, ed.). (1918). "The Poppy," from *The Complete Poetical Works of Francis Thompson*. Boni & Liveright, New York, N.Y.

Thondup, Tulku. (2000). *Boundless Healing: Meditation Exercises to Enlighten the Mind and Heal the Body*. Shambhala, Boston, p. 46.

Thoreau, Henry. (1854). *Walden*. Dover Publications, New York, N.Y. (1985).

———. (1906). *Journals*. Houghton Mifflin, Boston, Mass.

Thurber, James (Michael J. Rosen, ed.). *Collecting Himself: James Thurber on Writing and Writers, Humor, and Himself.* Harper & Row, New York, N.Y.

Trotsky, Leon. (1958). *Diary in Exile.* Harvard University Press, Cambridge, Mass.

Twain, Mark. (1906). *What is Man?* De Vinne Press, New York, N.Y.

———. (1996). *Following the Equator and Anti-Imperialist Essays.* Oxford University Press, New York, N.Y.

Valiente, Doreen. (1978). *Witchcraft for Tomorrow.* Phoenix Publishing, Custer, Wash.

Van Buren, Abigail. (16 May 1974). *Dear Abby* syndicated newspaper column.

Waite, A. E. (1973). *The Book of Black Magic and Ceremonial Magic.* Causeway Books, New York, N.Y.

Walker, Barbara G. (1983). *The Woman's Encyclopedia of Myths and Secrets.* HarperCollins, San Francisco, Calif.

Watkins, Calvert, ed. (1985). *The American Heritage Dictionary of Indo-European Roots (Revised).* Houghton Mifflin, Boston, Mass.

Weil, Simone. (1942). *New York Notebook* (written 1942; published 1950; repr. in *First and Last Notebooks.* Pt. 3, ed. by Richard Rees, 1970).

Weight Watchers International. *Weight Watchers' Little Book of Wisdom.* Weight Watchers International, Inc. N.p.

Wood, Robin. (1996). *When, Why . . . If.* Livingtree Book, Dearborn, Mich.

Index